The Advent of Grace

The Advent of Grace

Theological Briefs

BRADFORD MCCALL

WIPF & STOCK · Eugene, Oregon

THE ADVENT OF GRACE
Theological Briefs

Copyright © 2025 Bradford McCall. All rights reserved. Except for brief quotations in critical publications or reviews, no part of this book may be reproduced in any manner without prior written permission from the publisher. Write: Permissions, Wipf and Stock Publishers, 199 W. 8th Ave., Suite 3, Eugene, OR 97401.

Wipf & Stock
An Imprint of Wipf and Stock Publishers
199 W. 8th Ave., Suite 3
Eugene, OR 97401

www.wipfandstock.com

PAPERBACK ISBN: 978-1-7252-6759-6
HARDCOVER ISBN: 978-1-7252-6758-9
EBOOK ISBN: 978-1-7252-6760-2

VERSION NUMBER 04/17/25

Contents

About the Author | ix

Preface | xi

WEEK ONE

Week One, Day One | 1

Week One, Day Two | 7

Week One, Day Three | 13

Week One, Day Four | 19

Week One, Day Five | 25

Week One, Day Six | 31

Week One, Day Seven | 37

WEEK TWO

Week Two, Day Eight | 42

Week Two, Day Nine | 48

Week Two, Day Ten | 53

Week Two, Day Eleven | 58

Week Two, Day Twelve | 64

Week Two, Day Thirteen | 69

Week Two, Day Fourteen | 75

WEEK THREE

Week Three, Day Fifteen | 81

Week Three, Day Sixteen | 87

Week Three, Day Seventeen | 93

Week Three, Day Eighteen | 99

Week Three, Day Nineteen | 105

Week Three, Day Twenty | 110

Week Three, Day Twenty-One | 116

WEEK FOUR

Week Four, Day Twenty-Two | 122

Week Four, Day Twenty-Three | 128

Week Four, Day Twenty-Four | 134

Week Four, Day Twenty-Five | 139

Week Four, Day Twenty-Six | 145

Week Four, Day Twenty-Seven | 150

Week Four, Day Twenty-Eight | 155

WEEK FIVE

Week Five, Day Twenty-Nine | 161

Week Five, Day Thirty | 167

Week Five, Final Day | 173

About the Author

Dr. Bradford L. McCall holds a BS in biology (2000), four master's degrees in religion or philosophy (2005, MDiv from Asbury Theological Seminary; 2011, MA in church history and doctrine from Regent University; 2017, MA in systematic philosophy from Holy Apostles College and Seminary; 2020, MA in religious studies from Claremont School of Theology), and a PhD in comparative theology from Claremont School of Theology in Claremont, California, wherein his dissertation was entitled "Contingency and Divine Activity: Toward a Contemporary Conception of Divine Involvement in an Evolutionary World," which was successfully defended September 22, 2021. His *Doktorvater* and dissertation chair was the distinguished Dr. Philip Clayton. The other members of his committee were similarly distinguished in their areas of expertise: Dr. Ingolf U. Dalferth and Dr. Roland Faber. McCall has written or is in the process of writing nearly a dozen books: *A Modern Relation of Theology and Science Assisted by Emergence and Kenosis* (Eugene, OR: Wipf & Stock, 2018); *Evolution: Secular or Sacred?* (Eugene, OR: Wipf & Stock, 2020); *The God of Chance and Purpose: Divine Involvement in a Secular Evolutionary World* (Eugene, OR: Wipf & Stock, 2022); *Macroevolution, Contingency, and Divine Activity: Divine Involvement Through Uncontrolling, Amorepotent Love in an Evolutionary World* (Eugene, OR: Pickwick, 2023); as editor, *Reading Ruse: Michael Ruse on Darwinism, Science, and Faith*, with an autobiographical chapter by Michael Ruse (Eugene, OR: Cascade, 2024); *Triangulating Religion, Belief,*

About the Author

and *Faith in the Twenty-First Century*, the first of the Theological Briefs series (Eugene, OR: Wipf & Stock, 2025); and as editor, *Ruminating on Ruse: Key Themes in the Evolutionary Naturalism of Michael Ruse* (Eugene, OR: Cascade, forthcoming).

Preface

This title is the second in a series known as Theological Briefs. While one could write numerous dissertation-length manuscripts on these topics, the general concern of this new Theological Briefs series is to be just that: brief. However, this does not mean that serious academic reflection has been excised from these pages that follow. Rather, each book within this new series is calculated to be "bare bones" as much as possible without doing violence to the topic at hand. This means that ordinary filler words and filler material will be eclipsed in this series. We believe that this can be done across the broad range of theological topics if the authors consciously restrain themselves in their expository endeavors.

Regarding the derivation of the *Wash Me* prayer of confession, it has its rudiment of St. Peter Canisius, S.J., a mid-16th century Dutch Jesuit priest. The "Anima Christi" prayer, meaning "Soul of Christ," is a devotional prayer of Catholic origin that dates back to the first part of the 14th century. Its author is unknown, although it is often attributed to St. Ignatius Loyola. The "Christ be Near" prayer is rooted in the early Christian writings, particularly within the Eastern Orthodox tradition. The "Covenant" prayer has its origins popularly in the writings of John Wesley, although he originally adapted it from the Moravian Church in the mid-17th century. The" Gloria" prayer is of 4th century origin, as it was originally sung at the morning prayer, but not at mass. The "Glory Be" prayer was first used in Catholic traditions in the 4th century.

WEEK ONE, DAY ONE

The cross is something we can temporarily evade,
but we nevertheless take it up willingly,
even amid misgivings.
As a new month begins,
ponder whether you are
    willing, indeed eager, to see God work in new ways in your
        life,
    determined to trust God,
    willing to seek to give thanks to God in all things.

Opening Prayer

In the beginning—time remote—good Lord,
the heavens and the earth sprang forth from your overwhelming
    goodness;
you have promised to bring forth, moreover,
a new heaven and new earth in due time.
Grant to all your people, we beseech you, therefore,
    a firm conviction of your overwhelming goodness,
    a zeal to fully participate in whatever you intend for us,
    that we may be effective witnesses to the world
        in both word and in deed,
        as a people who steadfastly proclaim your love,
    through Christ, our savior and Lord.
Amen.

Prayer of Confession—Wash Me

See, oh merciful God, what return I,
your thankless servant, have made
for the innumerable favors
and the wonderful love you have shown me!
What wrongs I have done, what good left undone!
Wash away, I beg you, these faults and stains

with your precious blood, most kind redeemer,
and make up for my poverty by applying your merits.
Give me the protection I need to amend my life.
I give and surrender myself wholly to you,
and offer you all I possess,
with the prayer that you bestow your grace on me
so that I may be able to devote and employ
all the thinking power of my mind
and the strength of my body in your holy service,
who are God blessed for ever and ever.
Lord, enable me to see and find you in all things
and throughout my walks of life.
Amen.

Prayer for Illumination

Illuminator of all that exists,
as you called forth light in the opening moments of this natural world,
by the same power of your Spirit—we beseech you—
sweep thoroughly across our emptiness and darkness
insomuch that in reading and pondering scripture,
> we may more clearly see your way forward with respect to our lives
> and more clearly see how to proceed forward boldly in your name,

through Jesus Christ, our savior and Lord.
Amen.

scripture Reading: John 1:1–14

Prayer of Exhortation

Oh God of great deeds,
on the first day of the week
> you magnificently called forth light out of darkness;

you graciously raised Christ from the dead;
you powerfully created the church through the gift of Spirit.
Through these three witnesses,
you testify to us concerning your covenant love.
Grant that all people who worship you this day
may do so in spirit and in truth
and may present to you a living sacrifice
of praise and thanksgiving;
we praise you for the signs of your love revealed in the bread and the cup.
By these gifts grant us not only hope until we gather again
but also graciousness that we may share with others the fruits of this earth,
through Christ, our savior and Lord.
Amen.

Anima Christi

Soul of Christ, sanctify me.
Body of Christ, save me.
Blood of Christ, inebriate me.
Water from the side of Christ, wash me.
Passion of Christ, strengthen me.
Oh good Jesus, hear me.
Within your wounds hide me.
Separated from you let me never be.
From the evil one protect me.
At the hour of my death call me,
and close to you bid me,
that with your saints
I may praise you forever and ever.
Amen.

Christ Be Near

Christ be near at either hand;
Christ behind, before me stand.
Christ with me where'er I go;
Christ around, above, below.

Christ be in my heart and mind;
Christ within my mind enshrined.
Christ control my wayward heart;
Christ abide and ne'er depart.

Christ my light and only way;
Christ my lantern night and day.
Christ be my unchanging friend,
guide and shepherd to the end.

Christ be all my strength and might,
Christ my captain for the flight.
Christ fulfill my mind's desire;
Christ, ennoble and inspire.

Christ the king and Lord of all,
find me ready at his call;
Christ receive my service whole,
hand and body, heart and mind.

Christ the king of kings descend,
and of tyrants make an end;
Christ on us and all below,
concord, love, and peace bestow.

Thanks to him, who for our food
gives his sacrifice flesh and blood;
praises to him unceasingly rise,
Christ whose glory fills the skies.

Week One, Day One

Covenant Prayer

I am no longer my own, but thine.
Put me to what thou will,
rank me with whom thou will.
Put me to doing, put me to suffering.
Let me be employed by thee or laid aside for thee,
exalted for thee or brought low for thee.
Let me be full, let me be empty.
Let me have all things, let me have nothing.
I freely and heartily yield all things
to thy good pleasure and disposal.
And now, oh glorious and blessed God,
Father, Son, and Holy Spirit,
thou art mine, and I am thine.
So be it.
And the covenant which I have made on earth,
let it be ratified in heaven.
Amen.

The Gloria

Glory to God in the highest,
And on earth peace to men of good will.
We praise you.
We bless you.
We adore you.
We glorify you.
We give you thanks for your great glory,
oh Lord God, heavenly king, God the Father almighty.
Oh Lord Jesus Christ, the only begotten Son,
oh Lord God, lamb of God, Son of the Father,
    you who take away the sins of the world, have mercy on us;
    you who take away the sins of the world, receive our prayer;
    you who sit at the right hand of the Father, have mercy on us.

For you alone are holy.
You alone are the Lord.
You alone, oh Jesus Christ, are the most high,
together with the Holy Spirit in the glory of God the Father.
Amen.

Glory Be

Glory be to the Father
and to the Son
and to the Holy Spirit;
as it was in the beginning,
is now,
and ever shall be,
world without end.
Amen.

WEEK ONE, DAY TWO

Consistent and conscientious discipleship springs
from the assured knowledge that we are loved by God
and that all our devotion is a response to the goodness of God
    toward us.
Therefore, over the next three days,
we shall reflect on the nature of the gracious God of our universe,
who is the alpha and omega.
There are many competing deities in our world today.
Even if the forces that allure us are not identified as God,
let alone recognized as a false idol, that is still the situation in
    truth.
We do well, therefore, to reexamine regularly our understanding
    of God.

Opening Prayer

You alone are God.
You alone are holy.
You have made yourself known in the world.
You have made yourself known in faithful covenants:
    in the journey of Abraham and Sarah;
    in the great escape from slavery in Egypt;
    and the experience of judges, monarchs, and mighty
        prophets.
Above all, you revealed yourself in Jesus, your holy one,
and continually make known your presence in the power and
    might of the Spirit,
who is your sacred breath within us.
You alone are God.
You alone are holy.
Amen.

Prayer of Confession—Wash Me

See, oh merciful God, what return I,
your thankless servant, have made
for the innumerable favors
and the wonderful love you have shown me!
What wrongs I have done, what good left undone!
Wash away, I beg you, these faults and stains
with your precious blood, most kind redeemer,
and make up for my poverty by applying your merits.
Give me the protection I need to amend my life.
I give and surrender myself wholly to you,
and offer you all I possess,
with the prayer that you bestow your grace on me
so that I may be able to devote and employ
all the thinking power of my mind
and the strength of my body in your holy service,
who are God blessed for ever and ever.
Lord, enable me to see and find you in all things
and throughout my walks of life.
Amen.

Prayer for Illumination

Mighty God, our strength and hope,
you have not left us on our own, struggling to find you without
   direction.
Rather, you have come among us, and in the scriptures of the
   church,
you have given us a reliable record of your presence.
Open anew the meaning of what we read
that by the gifts of your Spirit,
we may be strengthened and sent forth to do your work in the
   world today,
through Jesus Christ, our savior and Lord.
Amen.

Week One, Day Two

scripture Reading: Psalm 96

Prayer of Exhortation

Remember, oh Lord, all for whom we prayed yesterday
while gathered together in corporate worship.
Teach us how best to serve them
with deeds of love and kindness.
Forgive us for those whom we neglected to raise up in prayer.
Help us to open our hearts to the needs of all.
Grant that what you taught us therein to do we may both ponder
   and perform.
Bind into one company of hope and one community of service
all that you have made and redeemed
by the sacrificial life and death of Jesus our Lord.
Amen.

Anima Christi

Soul of Christ, sanctify me.
Body of Christ, save me.
Blood of Christ, inebriate me.
Water from the side of Christ, wash me.
Passion of Christ, strengthen me.
Oh good Jesus, hear me.
Within your wounds hide me.
Separated from you let me never be.
From the evil one protect me.
At the hour of my death call me,
and close to you bid me,
that with your saints
I may praise you forever and ever.
Amen.

Christ Be Near

Christ be near at either hand;
Christ behind, before me stand.
Christ with me where'er I go;
Christ around, above, below.

Christ be in my heart and mind;
Christ within my mind enshrined.
Christ control my wayward heart;
Christ abide and ne'er depart.

Christ my light and only way;
Christ my lantern night and day.
Christ be my unchanging friend,
guide and shepherd to the end.

Christ be all my strength and might,
Christ my captain for the flight.
Christ fulfill my mind's desire;
Christ, ennoble and inspire.

Christ the king and Lord of all,
find me ready at his call;
Christ receive my service whole,
hand and body, heart and mind.

Christ the king of kings descend,
and of tyrants make an end;
Christ on us and all below,
concord, love, and peace bestow.

Thanks to him, who for our food
gives his sacrifice flesh and blood;
praises to him unceasingly rise,
Christ whose glory fills the skies.

Week One, Day Two

Covenant Prayer

I am no longer my own, but thine.
Put me to what thou will,
rank me with whom thou will.
Put me to doing, put me to suffering.
Let me be employed by thee or laid aside for thee,
exalted for thee or brought low for thee.
Let me be full, let me be empty.
Let me have all things, let me have nothing.
I freely and heartily yield all things
to thy good pleasure and disposal.
And now, oh glorious and blessed God,
Father, Son, and Holy Spirit,
thou art mine, and I am thine.
So be it.
And the covenant which I have made on earth,
let it be ratified in heaven.
Amen.

The Gloria

Glory to God in the highest,
And on earth peace to men of good will.
We praise you.
We bless you.
We adore you.
We glorify you.
We give you thanks for your great glory,
oh Lord God, heavenly king, God the Father almighty.
Oh Lord Jesus Christ, the only begotten Son,
oh Lord God, lamb of God, Son of the Father,
> you who take away the sins of the world, have mercy on us;
> you who take away the sins of the world, receive our prayer;
> you who sit at the right hand of the Father, have mercy on us.

For you alone are holy.
You alone are the Lord.
You alone, oh Jesus Christ, are the most high,
together with the Holy Spirit in the glory of God the Father.
Amen.

Glory Be

Glory be to the Father
and to the Son
and to the Holy Spirit;
as it was in the beginning,
is now,
and ever shall be,
world without end.
Amen.

WEEK ONE, DAY THREE

In Jesus, we find the most clear and complete glimpse of the eternal God that mortals are capable of experiencing.
The church has always contended that Jesus is far more than simply
a good moral teacher that ran afoul of conventional beliefs and ideas.
Jesus is nothing less than God among us (*Immanuel*).
In Jesus, we see the extent to which God will go to proclaim reconciliation
and to demonstrate a drastic reordering of life.
This is what it means
to say that Christ died in our stead, and rose for us.

Opening Prayer

Jesus, savior and sovereign, for our sakes, you brought to us your humility
and patience so that we might know more fully upon this earth the ways of heaven.
Willingly you allowed yourself to be given over to death in our hands.
Triumphantly, you conquered death for us and made us your friends rather than slaves of sin.
Drive from our hearts all ingratitude, all apathy, and all carelessness.
Into our hearts, thus emptied, pour out the fullness of your faithful witness,
that the world might behold in us some small sign of that eternal love
which existed between you, the Father, and the Spirit.
Amen.

Prayer of Confession—Wash Me

See, oh merciful God, what return I,
your thankless servant, have made
for the innumerable favors
and the wonderful love you have shown me!
What wrongs I have done, what good left undone!
Wash away, I beg you, these faults and stains
with your precious blood, most kind redeemer,
and make up for my poverty by applying your merits.
Give me the protection I need to amend my life.
I give and surrender myself wholly to you,
and offer you all I possess,
with the prayer that you bestow your grace on me
so that I may be able to devote and employ
all the thinking power of my mind
and the strength of my body in your holy service,
who are God blessed for ever and ever.
Lord, enable me to see and find you in all things
and throughout my walks of life.
Amen.

Prayer for Illumination

Jesus, the world's true light, in your ministry upon earth, you read from the scriptures and taught people the meaning of what they heard in the synagogues.
After your resurrection, you opened the scriptures again to those who walked up upon the Emmaus road with you. So now also enlighten us and give us the grace to do your will and to know the purpose of our lives through the power of your Spirit.
Amen.

Week One, Day Three

scripture Reading: Matthew 1:18–29

Prayer of Exhortation

Oh God, our rock and salvation, undergird us with your strength
lest we fall because we were trusting ourselves alone.
Assist with the Holy Spirit that we may abide in your love
and trust in your grace.
Spread upon us your transforming power;
overpower us with your goodwill and forgiveness
offered to us and all through Christ, our savior.
Amen.

Anima Christi

Soul of Christ, sanctify me.
Body of Christ, save me.
Blood of Christ, inebriate me.
Water from the side of Christ, wash me.
Passion of Christ, strengthen me.
Oh good Jesus, hear me.
Within your wounds hide me.
Separated from you let me never be.
From the evil one protect me.
At the hour of my death call me,
and close to you bid me,
that with your saints
I may praise you forever and ever.
Amen.

Christ Be Near

Christ be near at either hand;
Christ behind, before me stand.
Christ with me where'er I go;
Christ around, above, below.

Christ be in my heart and mind;
Christ within my mind enshrined.
Christ control my wayward heart;
Christ abide and ne'er depart.

Christ my light and only way;
Christ my lantern night and day.
Christ be my unchanging friend,
guide and shepherd to the end.

Christ be all my strength and might,
Christ my captain for the flight.
Christ fulfill my mind's desire;
Christ, ennoble and inspire.

Christ the king and Lord of all,
find me ready at his call;
Christ receive my service whole,
hand and body, heart and mind.

Christ the king of kings descend,
and of tyrants make an end;
Christ on us and all below,
concord, love, and peace bestow.

Thanks to him, who for our food
gives his sacrifice flesh and blood;
praises to him unceasingly rise,
Christ whose glory fills the skies.

Covenant Prayer

I am no longer my own, but thine.
Put me to what thou will,
rank me with whom thou will.
Put me to doing, put me to suffering.

Week One, Day Three

Let me be employed by thee or laid aside for thee,
exalted for thee or brought low for thee.
Let me be full, let me be empty.
Let me have all things, let me have nothing.
I freely and heartily yield all things
to thy good pleasure and disposal.
And now, oh glorious and blessed God,
Father, Son, and Holy Spirit,
thou art mine, and I am thine.
So be it.
And the covenant which I have made on earth,
let it be ratified in heaven.
Amen.

The Gloria

Glory to God in the highest,
And on earth peace to men of good will.
We praise you.
We bless you.
We adore you.
We glorify you.
We give you thanks for your great glory,
oh Lord God, heavenly king, God the Father almighty.
Oh Lord Jesus Christ, the only begotten Son,
oh Lord God, lamb of God, Son of the Father,
    you who take away the sins of the world, have mercy on us;
    you who take away the sins of the world, receive our prayer;
    you who sit at the right hand of the Father, have mercy on us.
For you alone are holy.
You alone are the Lord.
You alone, oh Jesus Christ, are the most high,
together with the Holy Spirit in the glory of God the Father.
Amen.

Glory Be

Glory be to the Father
and to the Son
and to the Holy Spirit;
as it was in the beginning,
is now,
and ever shall be,
world without end.
Amen.

WEEK ONE, DAY FOUR

The Holy Spirit is present and active among us.
The ascension of Jesus was not a loss, as if what he had done among us ceased.
Rather, it was a gain, for in the man from Nazareth, the power of God was made known.
And now, the work of the Holy Spirit and her power is let loose, crossing the entire world for all time.

Opening Prayer

Come, Holy Spirit; you are the sacred breath through which we have life.
You are the blessed wind by which we are refreshed and reinvigorated.
Distribute among us the Son's brightness, and also thereby clear our confusion
and dispel all notions that are evil in intent or in truth.
Then empower not only myself but all who seek your strength to do your will.
Blessed are you together with the Father and the Son, one God, in every age and beyond all time.
Amen.

Prayer of Confession—Wash Me

See, oh merciful God, what return I,
your thankless servant, have made
for the innumerable favors
and the wonderful love you have shown me!
What wrongs I have done, what good left undone!
Wash away, I beg you, these faults and stains
with your precious blood, most kind redeemer,
and make up for my poverty by applying your merits.
Give me the protection I need to amend my life.

I give and surrender myself wholly to you,
and offer you all I possess,
with the prayer that you bestow your grace on me
so that I may be able to devote and employ
all the thinking power of my mind
and the strength of my body in your holy service,
who are God blessed for ever and ever.
Lord, enable me to see and find you in all things
and throughout my walks of life.
Amen.

Prayer for Illumination

Spirit of God, unending and unfettered, by your divine assistance the scriptures came into being; by your divine assistance their messages are revealed to us.
Therefore, interpret the meaning of what we read
so that in our day we may be refreshed and renewed in witness
and in service to the world, in which you breathed life at the onset
of the natural world.
Amen.

scripture Reading: 2 Timothy 3:14–17

Prayer of Exhortation

In the middle of this week, good Lord,
assure me again of your presence in the midst of life.
Renew my strength and determination to do your will on earth,
even as it is done in heaven.
Save me from both myself and foes, as well as contentment
and from a vision that is too narrow.
Enable me to reach beyond my parish, into my community;
beyond my community, into every corner of your anguish world.
Help me to see even beyond this world

Week One, Day Four

into the vast expenses of the universe
that was created by your might.
This I ask through Christ Jesus,
through whom all things were made,
and in whom all things hold together.
Amen.

Anima Christi

Soul of Christ, sanctify me.
Body of Christ, save me.
Blood of Christ, inebriate me.
Water from the side of Christ, wash me.
Passion of Christ, strengthen me.
Oh good Jesus, hear me.
Within your wounds hide me.
Separated from you let me never be.
From the evil one protect me.
At the hour of my death call me,
and close to you bid me,
that with your saints
I may praise you forever and ever.
Amen.

Christ Be Near

Christ be near at either hand;
Christ behind, before me stand.
Christ with me where'er I go,
Christ around, above, below.

Christ be in my heart and mind;
Christ within my mind enshrined.
Christ control my wayward heart;
Christ abide and ne'er depart.

Christ my light and only way;
Christ my lantern night and day.
Christ be my unchanging friend,
guide and shepherd to the end.

Christ be all my strength and might,
Christ my captain for the flight.
Christ fulfill my mind's desire;
Christ, ennoble and inspire.

Christ the king and Lord of all,
find me ready at his call;
Christ receive my service whole,
hand and body, heart and mind.

Christ the king of kings descend,
and of tyrants make an end;
Christ on us and all below,
concord, love, and peace bestow.

Thanks to him, who for our food
gives his sacrifice flesh and blood;
praises to him unceasingly rise,
Christ whose glory fills the skies.

Covenant Prayer

I am no longer my own, but thine.
Put me to what thou will,
rank me with whom thou will.
Put me to doing, put me to suffering.

Week One, Day Four

Let me be employed by thee or laid aside for thee,
exalted for thee or brought low for thee.
Let me be full, let me be empty.
Let me have all things, let me have nothing.
I freely and heartily yield all things
to thy good pleasure and disposal.
And now, oh glorious and blessed God,
Father, Son, and Holy Spirit,
thou art mine, and I am thine.
So be it.
And the covenant which I have made on earth,
let it be ratified in heaven.
Amen.

The Gloria

Glory to God in the highest,
And on earth peace to men of good will.
We praise you.
We bless you.
We adore you.
We glorify you.
We give you thanks for your great glory,
oh Lord God, heavenly king, God the Father almighty.
Oh Lord Jesus Christ, the only begotten Son,
oh Lord God, lamb of God, Son of the Father,
    you who take away the sins of the world, have mercy on us;
    you who take away the sins of the world, receive our prayer;
    you who sit at the right hand of the Father, have mercy on us.
For you alone are holy.
You alone are the Lord.
You alone, oh Jesus Christ, are the most high,
together with the Holy Spirit in the glory of God the Father.
Amen.

Glory Be

Glory be to the Father
and to the Son
and to the Holy Spirit;
as it was in the beginning,
is now,
and ever shall be,
world without end.
Amen.

WEEK ONE, DAY FIVE

Over the past three days, we have studied God's grace.
Now we move on to God's sanctification process of our bodies
  and spirits.
We are told by Jesus to be perfect as God himself is perfect.
We are not expected, however,
to have the infinite capacity for goodness that God has.
However, we are expected up to live up to the amount of light
  that we have received.
Sanctification is not our good work for God,
but rather a good work that God does for us.
We offer ourselves at the altar of God to be living sacrifices
in the world today.
This constitutes our ability to be sanctified.

Opening Prayer

Accept me, oh Lord, as a sacrifice—alive and eager
to be used as you see fit.
I confess with shame that I'm all too readily conformed
to the image of this world.
Transform me by your mighty power, oh God, and renew my
  mind
    that I might discern your will,
      that I might know to do what is good, acceptable, and
        perfect.
This I pray, together with the whole church of God through the
  one
who was the perfect sacrifice, Jesus, savior of the world.
Amen.

Prayer of Confession—Wash Me

See, oh merciful God, what return I,
your thankless servant, have made
for the innumerable favors
and the wonderful love you have shown me!
What wrongs I have done, what good left undone!
Wash away, I beg you, these faults and stains
with your precious blood, most kind redeemer,
and make up for my poverty by applying your merits.
Give me the protection I need to amend my life.
I give and surrender myself wholly to you,
and offer you all I possess,
with the prayer that you bestow your grace on me
so that I may be able to devote and employ
all the thinking power of my mind
and the strength of my body in your holy service,
who are God blessed for ever and ever.
Lord, enable me to see and find you in all things
and throughout my walks of life.
Amen.

Prayer for Illumination

From the distraction in the midst of praying, save me, good Lord.
From presuming that I already know what the scriptures say fully,
 spare me.
Both in my mind and in my heart, put the force of your life-
 giving Spirit,
for the sake of Christ Jesus, my Lord.
Amen.

Week One, Day Five

scripture Reading: 1 Corinthians 15:35–49

Prayer of Exhortation

God, your glory calls your people to adoration daily.
Inspire all who plan to lead
in the worship of your congregation on the Lord's day.
Prepare my heart and the hearts of all your people
to receive their ministries with joy,
with gratitude to you,
and extravagant generosity toward others.
This we pray through Christ, the risen one.
Amen.

Anima Christi

Soul of Christ, sanctify me.
Body of Christ, save me.
Blood of Christ, inebriate me.
Water from the side of Christ, wash me.
Passion of Christ, strengthen me.
Oh good Jesus, hear me.
Within your wounds hide me.
Separated from you let me never be.
From the evil one protect me.
At the hour of my death call me,
and close to you bid me,
that with your saints
I may praise you forever and ever.
Amen.

Christ Be Near

Christ be near at either hand;
Christ behind, before me stand.
Christ with me where'er I go;

Christ around, above, below.
Christ be in my heart and mind;
Christ within my mind enshrined.
Christ control my wayward heart;
Christ abide and ne'er depart.

Christ my light and only way;
Christ my lantern night and day.
Christ be my unchanging friend,
guide and shepherd to the end.

Christ be all my strength and might,
Christ my captain for the flight.
Christ fulfill my mind's desire;
Christ, ennoble and inspire.

Christ the king and Lord of all,
find me ready at his call;
Christ receive my service whole,
hand and body, heart and mind.

Christ the king of kings descend,
and of tyrants make an end;
Christ on us and all below,
concord, love, and peace bestow.

Thanks to him, who for our food
gives his sacrifice flesh and blood;
praises to him unceasingly rise,
Christ whose glory fills the skies.

Covenant Prayer

I am no longer my own, but thine.
Put me to what thou will,
rank me with whom thou will.

Week One, Day Five

Put me to doing, put me to suffering.
Let me be employed by thee or laid aside for thee,
exalted for thee or brought low for thee.
Let me be full, let me be empty.
Let me have all things, let me have nothing.
I freely and heartily yield all things
to thy good pleasure and disposal.
And now, oh glorious and blessed God,
Father, Son, and Holy Spirit,
thou art mine, and I am thine.
So be it.
And the covenant which I have made on earth,
let it be ratified in heaven.
Amen.

The Gloria

Glory to God in the highest,
And on earth peace to men of good will.
We praise you.
We bless you.
We adore you.
We glorify you.
We give you thanks for your great glory,
oh Lord God, heavenly king, God the Father almighty.
Oh Lord Jesus Christ, the only begotten Son,
oh Lord God, lamb of God, Son of the Father,
    you who take away the sins of the world, have mercy on us;
    you who take away the sins of the world, receive our prayer;
    you who sit at the right hand of the Father, have mercy on us.
For you alone are holy.
You alone are the Lord.
You alone, oh Jesus Christ, are the most high,
together with the Holy Spirit in the glory of God the Father.
Amen.

Glory Be

Glory be to the Father
and to the Son
and to the Holy Spirit;
as it was in the beginning,
is now,
and ever shall be,
world without end.
Amen.

WEEK ONE, DAY SIX

Today we consider how our response of love for a loving God
shapes our lives and propels us forward into faithful action.
Micah (6:8) instructed us very simply to act (1) justly, (2) in love,
and (3) in mercy, as well as (4) to walk humbly before God.
However, this is not to say that justice and mercy can be separated because they cannot;
justice without mercy is legalistic, and even cruel.
Mercy without justice sacrifices fairness on the altar of
   sentimentality.
The proper answer is that God is both just and kind.
Humility is our response to a divine love toward us
and also is our witness to the power of God's love
that can be released through us to others.

Opening Prayer

Grant to us, oh God, the gift of walking humbly with you.
Give us the wisdom to know how best to temper justice with
   mercy,
to buttress mercy with justice, so that your will may be done on
   earth
as it is in heaven, through Christ, our judge, advocate, and
   mediator.
Amen.

Prayer of Confession—Wash Me

See, oh merciful God, what return I,
your thankless servant, have made
for the innumerable favors
and the wonderful love you have shown me!
What wrongs I have done, what good left undone!
Wash away, I beg you, these faults and stains
with your precious blood, most kind redeemer,

and make up for my poverty by applying your merits.
Give me the protection I need to amend my life.
I give and surrender myself wholly to you,
and offer you all I possess,
with the prayer that you bestow your grace on me
so that I may be able to devote and employ
all the thinking power of my mind
and the strength of my body in your holy service,
who are God blessed for ever and ever.
Lord, enable me to see and find you in all things
and throughout my walks of life.
Amen.

Prayer for Illumination

Great God, by the same Spirit who inspired the writing of the scriptures,
inspire also the right reading of them at this time
so that all who attentively regard these words may know the truth
and by it be set free,
through Christ, who himself is the way, the truth, and the life.
Amen.

scripture Reading: Psalm 119:105–12

Prayer of Exhortation

On this day, Lord Jesus, the flesh which you took upon yourself for us,
and for our salvation, was hung upon the cross by us.
There you suffered all things and died that we might have life
and have it in the abundance.
Blessed are you, Lord Jesus, for your astounding and abounding grace,
who with the Father and in the Spirit is,
through all time and in all eternity, one God.

Amen.

Anima Christi

Soul of Christ, sanctify me.
Body of Christ, save me.
Blood of Christ, inebriate me.
Water from the side of Christ, wash me.
Passion of Christ, strengthen me.
Oh good Jesus, hear me.
Within your wounds hide me.
Separated from you let me never be.
From the evil one protect me.
At the hour of my death call me,
and close to you bid me,
that with your saints
I may praise you forever and ever.
Amen.

Christ Be Near

Christ be near at either hand;
Christ behind, before me stand.
Christ with me where'er I go;
Christ around, above, below.

Christ be in my heart and mind;
Christ within my mind enshrined.
Christ control my wayward heart;
Christ abide and ne'er depart.

Christ my light and only way;
Christ my lantern night and day.
Christ be my unchanging friend,
guide and shepherd to the end.

Christ be all my strength and might,
Christ my captain for the flight.
Christ fulfill my mind's desire;
Christ, ennoble and inspire.

Christ the king and Lord of all,
find me ready at his call;
Christ receive my service whole,
hand and body, heart and mind.

Christ the king of kings descend,
and of tyrants make an end;
Christ on us and all below,
concord, love, and peace bestow.

Thanks to him, who for our food
gives his sacrifice flesh and blood;
praises to him unceasingly rise,
Christ whose glory fills the skies.

Covenant Prayer

I am no longer my own, but thine.
Put me to what thou will,
rank me with whom thou will.
Put me to doing, put me to suffering.
Let me be employed by thee or laid aside for thee,
exalted for thee or brought low for thee.
Let me be full, let me be empty.
Let me have all things, let me have nothing.
I freely and heartily yield all things
to thy good pleasure and disposal.
And now, oh glorious and blessed God,
Father, Son, and Holy Spirit,
thou art mine, and I am thine.

So be it.
And the covenant which I have made on earth,
let it be ratified in heaven.
Amen.

The Gloria

Glory to God in the highest,
And on earth peace to men of good will.
We praise you.
We bless you.
We adore you.
We glorify you.
We give you thanks for your great glory,
oh Lord God, heavenly king, God the Father almighty.
Oh Lord Jesus Christ, the only begotten Son,
oh Lord God, lamb of God, Son of the Father,
    you who take away the sins of the world, have mercy on us;
    you who take away the sins of the world, receive our prayer;
    you who sit at the right hand of the Father, have mercy on us.
For you alone are holy.
You alone are the Lord.
You alone, oh Jesus Christ, are the most high,
together with the Holy Spirit in the glory of God the Father.
Amen.

Glory Be

Glory be to the Father
and to the Son
and to the Holy Spirit;
as it was in the beginning,
is now,
and ever shall be,
world without end.
Amen.

WEEK ONE, DAY SEVEN

The apostle John instructs by reciting the words of our savior,
Jesus, that we might be full of joy,
so that Jesus' joy might be our joy moreover,
and thereby our joy might be complete in him (John 15:11).
The apostle Paul extends that thought insomuch
as we are to rejoice in all things (Phil 4:4–9).

Opening Prayer

Oh God, how happy are those whose strength is in you,
those who will go through life with you by their side.
In their hearts are the highways to Zion.
Cause us to be numbered with them, finding our dwelling place
    in you.
Now and hereafter grant us the delight of living in your house,
ever singing your praises.
Amen.

Prayer of Confession—Wash Me

See, oh merciful God, what return I,
your thankless servant, have made
for the innumerable favors
and the wonderful love you have shown me!
What wrongs I have done, what good left undone!
Wash away, I beg you, these faults and stains
with your precious blood, most kind redeemer,
and make up for my poverty by applying your merits.
Give me the protection I need to amend my life.
I give and surrender myself wholly to you,
and offer you all I possess,
with the prayer that you bestow your grace on me
so that I may be able to devote and employ
all the thinking power of my mind

and the strength of my body in your holy service,
who are God blessed for ever and ever.
Lord, enable me to see and find you in all things
and throughout my walks of life.
Amen.

Prayer for Illumination

Author of grace and our eternal guide,
    as we make our pilgrimage throughout this life, shed your
        light upon us lest we slip or go astray.
    Speak to us through the recorded witnesses of the church so
        that through the Spirit's interpretation of the scriptures,
        we may find direction and strength,
through Christ Jesus, the shepherd of our bodies.
Amen.

Scripture Reading: Philippians 4:4–9

Prayer of Exhortation

Prepare our hearts, oh Lord,
to join together with your whole congregation
to praise and serve you in the morn.
Reveal your presence to all who will gather in adoration and
    self-offering.
To those who cannot for good reason go gladly to your house,
give your strength and consolation so that they may know
of the concern of their community of faith.
Make us receptive to your word for us, and enable us to know
    your will.
Bind your people together in a shared faith, a common witness,
and compassionate service to the entire world,
through Christ Jesus, our savior and Lord.
Amen.

Week One, Day Seven

Anima Christi

Soul of Christ, sanctify me.
Body of Christ, save me.
Blood of Christ, inebriate me.
Water from the side of Christ, wash me.
Passion of Christ, strengthen me.
Oh good Jesus, hear me.
Within your wounds hide me.
Separated from you let me never be.
From the evil one protect me.
At the hour of my death call me,
and close to you bid me,
that with your saints
I may praise you forever and ever.
Amen.

Christ Be Near

Christ be near at either hand;
Christ behind, before me stand.
Christ with me where'er I go;
Christ around, above, below.

Christ be in my heart and mind;
Christ within my mind enshrined.
Christ control my wayward heart;
Christ abide and ne'er depart.

Christ my light and only way;
Christ my lantern night and day.
Christ be my unchanging friend,
guide and shepherd to the end.

Christ be all my strength and might,
Christ my captain for the flight.
Christ fulfill my mind's desire;
Christ, ennoble and inspire.

Christ the king and Lord of all,
find me ready at his call;
Christ receive my service whole,
hand and body, heart and mind.

Christ the king of kings descend,
and of tyrants make an end;
Christ on us and all below,
concord, love, and peace bestow.

Thanks to him, who for our food
gives his sacrifice flesh and blood;
praises to him unceasingly rise,
Christ whose glory fills the skies.

Covenant Prayer

I am no longer my own, but thine.
Put me to what thou will,
rank me with whom thou will.
Put me to doing, put me to suffering.
Let me be employed by thee or laid aside for thee,
exalted for thee or brought low for thee.
Let me be full, let me be empty.
Let me have all things, let me have nothing.
I freely and heartily yield all things
to thy good pleasure and disposal.
And now, oh glorious and blessed God,
Father, Son, and Holy Spirit,
thou art mine, and I am thine.
So be it.

Week One, Day Seven

And the covenant which I have made on earth,
let it be ratified in heaven.
Amen.

The Gloria

Glory to God in the highest,
And on earth peace to men of good will.
We praise you.
We bless you.
We adore you.
We glorify you.
We give you thanks for your great glory,
oh Lord God, heavenly king, God the Father almighty.
Oh Lord Jesus Christ, the only begotten Son,
oh Lord God, lamb of God, Son of the Father,
    you who take away the sins of the world, have mercy on us;
    you who take away the sins of the world, receive our prayer;
    you who sit at the right hand of the Father, have mercy on us.
For you alone are holy.
You alone are the Lord.
You alone, oh Jesus Christ, are the most high,
together with the Holy Spirit in the glory of God the Father.
Amen.

Glory Be

Glory be to the Father
and to the Son
and to the Holy Spirit;
as it was in the beginning,
is now,
and ever shall be,
world without end.
Amen.

WEEK TWO, DAY EIGHT

Christ is our peace (Eph 2:14). Peace is a fruit of the Spirit.
Peace is more than just an absence of immunity or hostility.
The Hebrew word translated as peace is *shalom*.
Shalom means wholeness and the perfecting of all that is broken or incomplete; it points to reconciliation and restitution.
Peace in this sense is far more than the absence of conflict or confusion.
Ultimately, peace is the restoration of God's original relationship with the natural world,
the overcoming of sin, and all resulting disruptions therefrom.

Opening Prayer

Most holy, undivided Trinity, within the complexity of your being there is unity;
yet from that unity flows forth diversity, and all taken together there is wholeness.
Share with us this mystery of your divine life so that we, despite our differences,
may not be at odds with one another, but rather may be at peace,
whole as you are whole, conscientious as trustees of your reconciling love.
Blessed are you in whose image we are made.
Amen.

Prayer of Confession—Wash Me

See, oh merciful God, what return I,
your thankless servant, have made
for the innumerable favors
and the wonderful love you have shown me!
What wrongs I have done, what good left undone!
Wash away, I beg you, these faults and stains
with your precious blood, most kind redeemer,

Week Two, Day Eight

and make up for my poverty by applying your merits.
Give me the protection I need to amend my life.
I give and surrender myself wholly to you,
and offer you all I possess,
with the prayer that you bestow your grace on me
so that I may be able to devote and employ
all the thinking power of my mind
and the strength of my body in your holy service,
who are God blessed for ever and ever.
Lord, enable me to see and find you in all things
and throughout my walks of life.
Amen.

Prayer for Illumination

Come, divine interpreter; present to us afresh the ancient words
lest we take them for granted as having small meaning for us.
Cause your Spirit to blow roundabout us, to breathe life within
   us;
and thus to refresh us and invigorate us for the work to be done
   in your name,
through Jesus Christ, our Lord.
Amen.

scripture Reading: John 16:31–33

Prayer of Exhortation

Oh God of great deeds,
on the first day of the week
   you magnificently called forth light out of darkness;
   you graciously raised Christ from the dead;
   you powerfully created the church through the gift of Spirit.
Through these three witnesses,
you testify to us concerning your covenant love.
Grant that all people who worship you this day

may do so in spirit and in truth
and may present to you a living sacrifice
of praise and thanksgiving;
we praise you for the signs of your love revealed in the bread and the cup.
By these gifts grant us not only hope until we gather again
but also graciousness that we may share with others the fruits of this earth,
through Christ, our savior and Lord.
Amen.

Anima Christi

Soul of Christ, sanctify me.
Body of Christ, save me.
Blood of Christ, inebriate me.
Water from the side of Christ, wash me.
Passion of Christ, strengthen me.
Oh good Jesus, hear me.
Within your wounds hide me.
Separated from you let me never be.
From the evil one protect me.
At the hour of my death call me,
and close to you bid me,
that with your saints
I may praise you forever and ever.
Amen.

Christ Be Near

Christ be near at either hand;
Christ behind, before me stand.
Christ with me where'er I go;
Christ around, above, below.

Week Two, Day Eight

Christ be in my heart and mind;
Christ within my mind enshrined.
Christ control my wayward heart;
Christ abide and ne'er depart.

Christ my light and only way;
Christ my lantern night and day.
Christ be my unchanging friend,
guide and shepherd to the end.

Christ be all my strength and might,
Christ my captain for the flight.
Christ fulfill my mind's desire;
Christ, ennoble and inspire.

Christ the king and Lord of all,
find me ready at his call;
Christ receive my service whole,
hand and body, heart and mind.

Christ the king of kings descend,
and of tyrants make an end;
Christ on us and all below,
concord, love, and peace bestow.

Thanks to him, who for our food
gives his sacrifice flesh and blood;
praises to him unceasingly rise,
Christ whose glory fills the skies.

Covenant Prayer

I am no longer my own, but thine.
Put me to what thou will,
rank me with whom thou will.
Put me to doing, put me to suffering.

Let me be employed by thee or laid aside for thee,
exalted for thee or brought low for thee.
Let me be full, let me be empty.
Let me have all things, let me have nothing.
I freely and heartily yield all things
to thy good pleasure and disposal.
And now, oh glorious and blessed God,
Father, Son, and Holy Spirit,
thou art mine, and I am thine.
So be it.
And the covenant which I have made on earth,
let it be ratified in heaven.
Amen.

The Gloria

Glory to God in the highest,
And on earth peace to men of good will.
We praise you.
We bless you.
We adore you.
We glorify you.
We give you thanks for your great glory,
oh Lord God, heavenly king, God the Father almighty.
Oh Lord Jesus Christ, the only begotten Son,
oh Lord God, lamb of God, Son of the Father,
    you who take away the sins of the world, have mercy on us;
    you who take away the sins of the world, receive our prayer;
    you who sit at the right hand of the Father, have mercy on us.
For you alone are holy.
You alone are the Lord.
You alone, oh Jesus Christ, are the most high,
together with the Holy Spirit in the glory of God the Father.
Amen.

Week Two, Day Eight

Glory Be

Glory be to the Father
and to the Son
and to the Holy Spirit;
as it was in the beginning,
is now,
and ever shall be,
world without end.
Amen.

WEEK TWO, DAY NINE

Christ bestows us patience as a fruit of the Spirit.
We need to continually request that God grant us patience,
as well as the gift of trust that undergirds patience.
Pray for trust in the graciousness of God whose schedule is
not always accommodating to ours,
but whose will is always directed toward our good.

Opening Prayer

Eternal God, you cannot be constrained by our ways of counting time.
Grant us, therefore, patient endurance and steadfast trust
so that we may wait for you without faltering
and while witnessing to others,
may serve you without hesitation in good times or ill,
for the sake of Christ Jesus, your faithful witness.
Amen.

Prayer of Confession—Wash Me

See, oh merciful God, what return I,
your thankless servant, have made
for the innumerable favors
and the wonderful love you have shown me!
What wrongs I have done, what good left undone!
Wash away, I beg you, these faults and stains
with your precious blood, most kind redeemer,
and make up for my poverty by applying your merits.
Give me the protection I need to amend my life.
I give and surrender myself wholly to you,
and offer you all I possess,
with the prayer that you bestow your grace on me
so that I may be able to devote and employ
all the thinking power of my mind

and the strength of my body in your holy service,
who are God blessed for ever and ever.
Lord, enable me to see and find you in all things
and throughout my walks of life.
Amen.

Prayer for Illumination

Merciful God, take from us all hardness of heart and dimness of
  mind.
Move from us our reluctance to know and do your will.
Fill the church with your Spirit as on the day of Pentecost long
  ago,
and open the scriptures for the benefit of your people of every
  language, tribe, and nation,
through Jesus, who is the Word made flesh.
Amen.

scripture Reading: Colossians 3:12–15

Prayer of Exhortation

Remember, oh Lord, all for whom we prayed yesterday
while gathered together in corporate worship.
Teach us how best to serve them
with deeds of love and kindness.
Forgive us for those whom we neglected to raise up in prayer.
Help us to open our hearts to the needs of all.
Grant that what you taught us therein to do we may both ponder
  and perform.
Bind into one company of hope and one community of service
all that you have made and redeemed
by the sacrificial life and death of Jesus our Lord.
Amen.

Anima Christi

Soul of Christ, sanctify me.
Body of Christ, save me.
Blood of Christ, inebriate me.
Water from the side of Christ, wash me.
Passion of Christ, strengthen me.
Oh good Jesus, hear me.
Within your wounds hide me.
Separated from you let me never be.
From the evil one protect me.
At the hour of my death call me,
and close to you bid me,
that with your saints
I may praise you forever and ever.
Amen.

Christ Be Near

Christ be near at either hand;
Christ behind, before me stand.
Christ with me where'er I go;
Christ around, above, below.

Christ be in my heart and mind;
Christ within my mind enshrined.
Christ control my wayward heart;
Christ abide and ne'er depart.

Christ my light and only way;
Christ my lantern night and day.
Christ be my unchanging friend,
guide and shepherd to the end.

Week Two, Day Nine

Christ be all my strength and might,
Christ my captain for the flight.
Christ fulfill my mind's desire;
Christ, ennoble and inspire.

Christ the king and Lord of all,
find me ready at his call;
Christ receive my service whole,
hand and body, heart and mind.

Christ the king of kings descend,
and of tyrants make an end;
Christ on us and all below,
concord, love, and peace bestow.

Thanks to him, who for our food
gives his sacrifice flesh and blood;
praises to him unceasingly rise,
Christ whose glory fills the skies.

Covenant Prayer

I am no longer my own, but thine.
Put me to what thou will,
rank me with whom thou will.
Put me to doing, put me to suffering.
Let me be employed by thee or laid aside for thee,
exalted for thee or brought low for thee.
Let me be full, let me be empty.
Let me have all things, let me have nothing.
I freely and heartily yield all things
to thy good pleasure and disposal.
And now, oh glorious and blessed God,
Father, Son, and Holy Spirit,
thou art mine, and I am thine.
So be it.

And the covenant which I have made on earth,
let it be ratified in heaven.
Amen.

The Gloria

Glory to God in the highest,
And on earth peace to men of good will.
We praise you.
We bless you.
We adore you.
We glorify you.
We give you thanks for your great glory,
oh Lord God, heavenly king, God the Father almighty.
Oh Lord Jesus Christ, the only begotten Son,
oh Lord God, lamb of God, Son of the Father,
    you who take away the sins of the world, have mercy on us;
    you who take away the sins of the world, receive our prayer;
    you who sit at the right hand of the Father, have mercy on us.
For you alone are holy.
You alone are the Lord.
You alone, oh Jesus Christ, are the most high,
together with the Holy Spirit in the glory of God the Father.
Amen.

Glory Be

Glory be to the Father
and to the Son
and to the Holy Spirit;
as it was in the beginning,
is now,
and ever shall be,
world without end.
Amen.

WEEK TWO, DAY TEN

Today we consider kindness as a fruit of the Spirit.
True kindness is a response of the heart, not a resolve of the will.
Kindness from God toward us is the ultimate idea that results
in and engenders our genuine kindness toward others.
In pondering our ability to show kindness toward others,
it is wise for us to ask what kindness God has shown us in
forgiving our sins, and in granting us hope for life to the fullest.
We can best express our gratitude for God's gifts of kindness
toward us by expressing genuine kindness toward other humans.

Opening Prayer

Oh generous God, what goodness you show us day by day.
Your mercies never come to an end. Like manna from heaven,
they are renewed every morning. Great is your faithfulness,
oh God. It is from you, then, that we learn kindness in hospitality.
It is to honor and thank you that we extend to others what you
    extend to us.
Accept what we offer as a sacrifice of praise and thanksgiving,
and grant that we may continue in your kindness forever,
through Christ, who, upon the cross,
made known the most fully the extent of your perfect love.
Amen.

Prayer of Confession—Wash Me

See, oh merciful God, what return I,
your thankless servant, have made
for the innumerable favors
and the wonderful love you have shown me!
What wrongs I have done, what good left undone!
Wash away, I beg you, these faults and stains
with your precious blood, most kind redeemer,
and make up for my poverty by applying your merits.

Give me the protection I need to amend my life.
I give and surrender myself wholly to you,
and offer you all I possess,
with the prayer that you bestow your grace on me
so that I may be able to devote and employ
all the thinking power of my mind
and the strength of my body in your holy service,
who are God blessed for ever and ever.
Lord, enable me to see and find you in all things
and throughout my walks of life.
Amen.

Prayer for Illumination

Teach us, oh God, by the work of your Spirit,
what you are saying to us today.
Thereby enable us to learn to delight in your love
and to walk in your ways,
through Christ Jesus, the redeemer of the world.
Amen.

scripture Reading: James 2:10–13

Prayer of Exhortation

Oh God, our rock and salvation, undergird us with your strength
lest we fall because we were trusting ourselves alone.
Assist with the Holy Spirit that we may abide in your love
and trust in your grace.
Spread upon us your transforming power;
overpower us with your goodwill and forgiveness
offered to us and all through Christ, our savior.

Week Two, Day Ten

Anima Christi

Soul of Christ, sanctify me.
Body of Christ, save me.
Blood of Christ, inebriate me.
Water from the side of Christ, wash me.
Passion of Christ, strengthen me.
Oh good Jesus, hear me.
Within your wounds hide me.
Separated from you let me never be.
From the evil one protect me.
At the hour of my death call me,
and close to you bid me,
that with your saints
I may praise you forever and ever.
Amen.

Christ Be Near

Christ be near at either hand;
Christ behind, before me stand.
Christ with me where'er I go,
Christ around, above, below.

Christ be in my heart and mind;
Christ within my mind enshrined.
Christ control my wayward heart;
Christ abide and ne'er depart.

Christ my light and only way;
Christ my lantern night and day.
Christ be my unchanging friend,
guide and shepherd to the end.

Christ be all my strength and might,
Christ my captain for the flight.
Christ fulfill my mind's desire;
Christ, ennoble and inspire.

Christ the king and Lord of all,
find me ready at his call;
Christ receive my service whole,
hand and body, heart and mind.

Christ the king of kings descend,
and of tyrants make an end;
Christ on us and all below,
concord, love, and peace bestow.

Thanks to him, who for our food
gives his sacrifice flesh and blood;
praises to him unceasingly rise,
Christ whose glory fills the skies.

Covenant Prayer

I am no longer my own, but thine.
Put me to what thou will,
rank me with whom thou will.
Put me to doing, put me to suffering.
Let me be employed by thee or laid aside for thee,
exalted for thee or brought low for thee.
Let me be full, let me be empty.
Let me have all things, let me have nothing.
I freely and heartily yield all things
to thy good pleasure and disposal.
And now, oh glorious and blessed God,
Father, Son, and Holy Spirit,
thou art mine, and I am thine.
So be it.

Week Two, Day Ten

And the covenant which I have made on earth,
let it be ratified in heaven.
Amen.

The Gloria

Glory to God in the highest,
And on earth peace to men of good will.
We praise you.
We bless you.
We adore you.
We glorify you.
We give you thanks for your great glory,
oh Lord God, heavenly king, God the Father almighty.
Oh Lord Jesus Christ, the only begotten Son,
oh Lord God, lamb of God, Son of the Father,
    you who take away the sins of the world, have mercy on us;
    you who take away the sins of the world, receive our prayer;
    you who sit at the right hand of the Father, have mercy on us.
For you alone are holy.
You alone are the Lord.
You alone, oh Jesus Christ, are the most high,
together with the Holy Spirit in the glory of God the Father.
Amen.

Glory Be

Glory be to the Father
and to the Son
and to the Holy Spirit;
as it was in the beginning,
is now,
and ever shall be,
world without end.
Amen.

WEEK TWO, DAY ELEVEN

God loves a cheerful giver (2 Cor 9:7).
The gospel often sounds like sheer foolishness,
when judged by human reason.
God does not seem to care at all about how much we earn,
although it is by this measure that people in our society largely judge one another.
Rather, God is concerned about how much we have to give away.
How truly happy are those who learned the lesson that it
matters not how much we have until we know how much we can give away.
Ask yourself this day: Am I a cheerful giver or a reluctant one?
When giving something away do I ever quietly utter this prayer
to God and ask him to help me give away even more?
How often do we recount John Wesley's rule that we are to earn all we can,
save all we can, and give away all we can?

Opening Prayer

Oh God of heaven, by coming to earth to dwell among us,
you have demonstrated the greatest generosity possible.
Enable us to see in the manger, and in the cross,
the joy of giving ourselves fully in your service.
Take away from us the fear that if we give away what we have,
we'll have less or even nothing. Enable us to learn the lesson
that those who would save their lives, lose them,
while those who lose their lives for the sake of the gospel truly find them.
We pray this through him who taught us both in word and in deed,
through Christ Jesus, the perfect offering.
Amen.

Week Two, Day Eleven

Prayer of Confession—Wash Me

See, oh merciful God, what return I,
your thankless servant, have made
for the innumerable favors
and the wonderful love you have shown me!
What wrongs I have done, what good left undone!
Wash away, I beg you, these faults and stains
with your precious blood, most kind redeemer,
and make up for my poverty by applying your merits.
Give me the protection I need to amend my life.
I give and surrender myself wholly to you,
and offer you all I possess,
with the prayer that you bestow your grace on me
so that I may be able to devote and employ
all the thinking power of my mind
and the strength of my body in your holy service,
who are God blessed for ever and ever.
Lord, enable me to see and find you in all things
and throughout my walks of life.
Amen.

Prayer for Illumination

God, our blessing and helper, in the scriptures,
you have given us the resources to find the way of life
you intend for us. By your Spirit's faithfulness,
enable us to understand this way without distortion
and to walk in it without timidity,
through Christ Jesus, our savior.
Amen.

The Advent of Grace

Scripture Reading: 2 Timothy 1:3–7

Prayer of Exhortation

In the middle of this week, good Lord,
assure me again of your presence in the midst of life.
Renew my strength and determination to do your will on earth,
even as it is done in heaven.
Save me from both myself and foes, as well as contentment
and from a vision that is too narrow.
Enable me to reach beyond my parish, into my community;
beyond my community, into every corner of your anguish world.
Help me to see even beyond this world
into the vast expenses of the universe
that was created by your might.
This I ask through Christ Jesus,
through whom all things were made,
and in whom all things hold together.
Amen.

Anima Christi

Soul of Christ, sanctify me.
Body of Christ, save me.
Blood of Christ, inebriate me.
Water from the side of Christ, wash me.
Passion of Christ, strengthen me.
Oh good Jesus, hear me.
Within your wounds hide me.
Separated from you let me never be.
From the evil one protect me.
At the hour of my death call me,
and close to you bid me,
that with your saints
I may praise you forever and ever.
Amen.

Christ Be Near

Christ be near at either hand;
Christ behind, before me stand.
Christ with me where'er I go;
Christ around, above, below.

Christ be in my heart and mind;
Christ within my mind enshrined.
Christ control my wayward heart;
Christ abide and ne'er depart.

Christ my light and only way;
Christ my lantern night and day.
Christ be my unchanging friend,
guide and shepherd to the end.

Christ be all my strength and might,
Christ my captain for the flight.
Christ fulfill my mind's desire;
Christ, ennoble and inspire.

Christ the king and Lord of all,
find me ready at his call;
Christ receive my service whole,
hand and body, heart and mind.

Christ the king of kings descend,
and of tyrants make an end;
Christ on us and all below,
concord, love, and peace bestow.

Thanks to him, who for our food
gives his sacrifice flesh and blood;
praises to him unceasingly rise,
Christ whose glory fills the skies.

Covenant Prayer

I am no longer my own, but thine.
Put me to what thou will,
rank me with whom thou will.
Put me to doing, put me to suffering.
Let me be employed by thee or laid aside for thee,
exalted for thee or brought low for thee.
Let me be full, let me be empty.
Let me have all things, let me have nothing.
I freely and heartily yield all things
to thy good pleasure and disposal.
And now, oh glorious and blessed God,
Father, Son, and Holy Spirit,
thou art mine, and I am thine.
So be it.
And the covenant which I have made on earth,
let it be ratified in heaven.
Amen.

The Gloria

Glory to God in the highest,
And on earth peace to men of good will.
We praise you.
We bless you.
We adore you.
We glorify you.
We give you thanks for your great glory,
oh Lord God, heavenly king, God the Father almighty.
Oh Lord Jesus Christ, the only begotten Son,
oh Lord God, lamb of God, Son of the Father,
> you who take away the sins of the world, have mercy on us;
> you who take away the sins of the world, receive our prayer;
> you who sit at the right hand of the Father, have mercy on us.

For you alone are holy.

Week Two, Day Eleven

You alone are the Lord.
You alone, oh Jesus Christ, are the most high,
together with the Holy Spirit in the glory of God the Father.
Amen.

Glory Be

Glory be to the Father
and to the Son
and to the Holy Spirit;
as it was in the beginning,
is now,
and ever shall be,
world without end.
Amen.

WEEK TWO, DAY TWELVE

Today we examine faithfulness as a fruit of the Spirit.
Faithfulness begins with God and his being itself.
Because God is faithful, we can be faithful.
The utter reliability of God constitutes the basis for the faithfulness of God.
Once we reckon it true—that is, the dependability of God—
we can join confidently in the covenant that God offers to us.
On this day, we pray for the grace to trust in God's goodness,
to keep our vows with fidelity,
and to be those who instruct others in the way of truth.

Opening Prayer

God of all ages, in every time and place, you have been steadfast.
Your faithfulness endures without fail from generation to generation.
So then, bind to yourself the hearts of your covenant people
so that all who have promised fidelity to the gospel may fulfill their vowels.
Preserve your church, not only from the renunciation or neglect of faith
but also from the faith that calls forth from others contempt rather than conversion.

Prayer of Confession—Wash Me

See, oh merciful God, what return I,
your thankless servant, have made
for the innumerable favors
and the wonderful love you have shown me!
What wrongs I have done, what good left undone!
Wash away, I beg you, these faults and stains
with your precious blood, most kind redeemer,
and make up for my poverty by applying your merits.
Give me the protection I need to amend my life.

Week Two, Day Twelve

I give and surrender myself wholly to you,
and offer you all I possess,
with the prayer that you bestow your grace on me
so that I may be able to devote and employ
all the thinking power of my mind
and the strength of my body in your holy service,
who are God blessed for ever and ever.
Lord, enable me to see and find you in all things
and throughout my walks of life.
Amen.

Prayer for Illumination

You, oh God, gave ancient writers the grace to record
their experiences of your work in their midst.
So also give us the grace to discover your hand in our day as well,
as the scriptures are read and pondered.
Illuminate us with the Spirit so that we may see
more clearly your truth and your will for us,
through the merits and mediation of Christ, our Lord.
Amen.

scripture Reading: 1 Corinthians 2:10–16

Prayer of Exhortation

God, your glory calls your people to adoration daily.
Inspire all who plan to lead
in the worship of your congregation on the Lord's day.
Prepare my heart and the hearts of all your people
to receive their ministries with joy,
with gratitude to you,
and extravagant generosity toward others.
This we pray through Christ, the risen one.
Amen.

Anima Christi

Soul of Christ, sanctify me.
Body of Christ, save me.
Blood of Christ, inebriate me.
Water from the side of Christ, wash me.
Passion of Christ, strengthen me.
Oh good Jesus, hear me.
Within your wounds hide me.
Separated from you let me never be.
From the evil one protect me.
At the hour of my death call me,
and close to you bid me,
that with your saints
I may praise you forever and ever.
Amen.

Christ Be Near

Christ be near at either hand;
Christ behind, before me stand.
Christ with me where'er I go;
Christ around, above, below.

Christ be in my heart and mind;
Christ within my mind enshrined.
Christ control my wayward heart;
Christ abide and ne'er depart.

Christ my light and only way;
Christ my lantern night and day.
Christ be my unchanging friend,
guide and shepherd to the end.

Week Two, Day Twelve

Christ be all my strength and might,
Christ my captain for the flight.
Christ fulfill my mind's desire;
Christ, ennoble and inspire.

Christ the king and Lord of all,
find me ready at his call;
Christ receive my service whole,
hand and body, heart and mind.

Christ the king of kings descend,
and of tyrants make an end;
Christ on us and all below,
concord, love, and peace bestow.

Thanks to him, who for our food
gives his sacrifice flesh and blood;
praises to him unceasingly rise,
Christ whose glory fills the skies.

Covenant Prayer

I am no longer my own, but thine.
Put me to what thou will,
rank me with whom thou will.
Put me to doing, put me to suffering.
Let me be employed by thee or laid aside for thee,
exalted for thee or brought low for thee.
Let me be full, let me be empty.
Let me have all things, let me have nothing.
I freely and heartily yield all things
to thy good pleasure and disposal.
And now, oh glorious and blessed God,
Father, Son, and Holy Spirit,
thou art mine, and I am thine.
So be it.

And the covenant which I have made on earth,
let it be ratified in heaven.
Amen.

The Gloria

Glory to God in the highest,
And on earth peace to men of good will.
We praise you.
We bless you.
We adore you.
We glorify you.
We give you thanks for your great glory,
oh Lord God, heavenly king, God the Father almighty.
Oh Lord Jesus Christ, the only begotten Son,
oh Lord God, lamb of God, Son of the Father,
> you who take away the sins of the world, have mercy on us;
> you who take away the sins of the world, receive our prayer;
> you who sit at the right hand of the Father, have mercy on us.

For you alone are holy.
You alone are the Lord.
You alone, oh Jesus Christ, are the most high,
together with the Holy Spirit in the glory of God the Father.
Amen.

Glory Be

Glory be to the Father
and to the Son
and to the Holy Spirit;
as it was in the beginning,
is now,
and ever shall be,
world without end.
Amen.

WEEK TWO, DAY THIRTEEN

Today we consider gentleness as a fruit of the Spirit.
From birth it seems as though we humans know how to instinctively be harsh and even cruel.
Most of us also have mastered well the skills of sarcasm and superiority.
On other hand, gentleness seems like something that we have to learn.
And this is particularly so when dealing with others who oppose us.
Paul the apostle asked the Corinthians, "What would you prefer? Am I to come to you with a stick, or with love and a spirit of gentleness?"
It seems self-evident what the answer that to that question is.
Indeed, in all interactions it seems self-evident that gentleness is the best pathway forward.

Opening Prayer

Give grace, oh Lord Jesus, as I seek your way so that I may grow more and more into your likeness and that I may bear your ensign.
Through this time of daily devotion, instill in me your own gentleness,
quiet my alarm, and enable me to rest confidently in your wisdom.
Grant these things by the power of your Spirit, I beseech you.
Amen.

Prayer of Confession—Wash Me

See, oh merciful God, what return I,
your thankless servant, have made
for the innumerable favors
and the wonderful love you have shown me!

What wrongs I have done, what good left undone!
Wash away, I beg you, these faults and stains
with your precious blood, most kind redeemer,
and make up for my poverty by applying your merits.
Give me the protection I need to amend my life.
I give and surrender myself wholly to you,
and offer you all I possess,
with the prayer that you bestow your grace on me
so that I may be able to devote and employ
all the thinking power of my mind
and the strength of my body in your holy service,
who are God blessed for ever and ever.
Lord, enable me to see and find you in all things
and throughout my walks of life.
Amen.

Prayer for Illumination

Eternal God, you have willingly come to me in the confines
of my little world to stretch me in order to open before me un-
 imagined paths.
Through the studies of the scriptures, continue to work in and
 through me
so that by the power of your Spirit, I may more fully become what
you intend for me to be, through Christ, the redeemer of all
 things.
Amen.

scripture Reading: Romans 11:33–36

Prayer of Exhortation

On this day, Lord Jesus, the flesh which you took upon yourself
 for us,
and for our salvation, was hung upon the cross by us.
There you suffered all things and died that we might have life

Week Two, Day Thirteen

and have it in the abundance.
Blessed are you, Lord Jesus, for your astounding and abounding
 grace,
who with the Father and in the Spirit is,
through all time and in all eternity, one God.
Amen.

Anima Christi

Soul of Christ, sanctify me.
Body of Christ, save me.
Blood of Christ, inebriate me.
Water from the side of Christ, wash me.
Passion of Christ, strengthen me.
Oh good Jesus, hear me.
Within your wounds hide me.
Separated from you let me never be.
From the evil one protect me.
At the hour of my death call me,
and close to you bid me,
that with your saints
I may praise you forever and ever.
Amen.

Christ Be Near

Christ be near at either hand;
Christ behind, before me stand.
Christ with me where'er I go;
Christ around, above, below.

Christ be in my heart and mind;
Christ within my mind enshrined.
Christ control my wayward heart;
Christ abide and ne'er depart.
Christ my light and only way;

Christ my lantern night and day.
Christ be my unchanging friend,
guide and shepherd to the end.

Christ be all my strength and might,
Christ my captain for the flight.
Christ fulfill my mind's desire;
Christ, ennoble and inspire.

Christ the king and Lord of all,
find me ready at his call;
Christ receive my service whole,
hand and body, heart and mind.

Christ the king of kings descend,
and of tyrants make an end;
Christ on us and all below,
concord, love, and peace bestow.

Thanks to him, who for our food
gives his sacrifice flesh and blood;
praises to him unceasingly rise,
Christ whose glory fills the skies.

Covenant Prayer

I am no longer my own, but thine.
Put me to what thou wilt,
rank me with whom thou wilt.
Put me to doing, put me to suffering.
Let me be employed by thee or laid aside for thee,
exalted for thee or brought low for thee.
Let me be full, let me be empty.
Let me have all things, let me have nothing.
I freely and heartily yield all things
to thy good pleasure and disposal.

Week Two, Day Thirteen

And now, oh glorious and blessed God,
Father, Son, and Holy Spirit,
thou art mine, and I am thine.
So be it.
And the covenant which I have made on earth,
let it be ratified in heaven.
Amen.

The Gloria

Glory to God in the highest,
And on earth peace to men of good will.
We praise you.
We bless you.
We adore you.
We glorify you.
We give you thanks for your great glory,
oh Lord God, heavenly king, God the Father almighty.
Oh Lord Jesus Christ, the only begotten Son,
oh Lord God, lamb of God, Son of the Father,
    you who take away the sins of the world, have mercy on us;
    you who take away the sins of the world, receive our prayer;
    you who sit at the right hand of the Father, have mercy on us.
For you alone are holy.
You alone are the Lord.
You alone, oh Jesus Christ, are the most high,
together with the Holy Spirit in the glory of God the Father.
Amen.

Glory Be

Glory be to the Father
and to the Son
and to the Holy Spirit;
as it was in the beginning,
is now,
and ever shall be,
world without end.
Amen.

WEEK TWO, DAY FOURTEEN

Today we consider self-control as a fruit of the Spirit.
Neither self-control nor self-discipline are a favorite pursuit
for most of us people in the world today.
Self-indulgence is by far the more popular pursuit—
that is, much less work and certainly more fun at least in the
  short term.
In 1 Corinthians, Paul seeks to motivate us by comparing
the short- and long-term view of things.
Let us honestly answer these questions today:
  In what parts of my life do I have sufficient self-control,
  and what areas do I need to improve?
  Am I determined to bring about improvement in these areas
    with the help of God?

Opening Prayer

God almighty, you call us to ever more devotion and service.
Help us to have under control every impulse that distracts us
  from
loving you and every impediment that disrupts our work for you.
As a trainer prepares an athlete for a contest,
discipline us so that we may grow and strengthen in endurance
and thereafter may receive the crown of life from your hand.
Enable us to see value in all things, be they good for me or
apparently wicked, so that I may grow in righteousness.

Prayer of Confession—Wash Me

See, oh merciful God, what return I,
your thankless servant, have made
for the innumerable favors
and the wonderful love you have shown me!
What wrongs I have done, what good left undone!
Wash away, I beg you, these faults and stains

with your precious blood, most kind redeemer,
and make up for my poverty by applying your merits.
Give me the protection I need to amend my life.
I give and surrender myself wholly to you,
and offer you all I possess,
with the prayer that you bestow your grace on me
so that I may be able to devote and employ
all the thinking power of my mind
and the strength of my body in your holy service,
who are God blessed for ever and ever.
Lord, enable me to see and find you in all things
and throughout my walks of life.
Amen.

Prayer for Illumination

Without your aid, God, I cannot begin to understand you. However, because you would not have yourself be unknown, you have given us a record of your work from creation onward, set down for us by poets, prophets, apostles, and evangelists. Give to me what I need and strengthen me to accomplish your purposes for me by reading this record and pondering it.
Amen.

scripture Reading: 1 Corinthians 9:24–27

Prayer of Exhortation

Prepare our hearts, oh Lord,
to join together with your whole congregation
to praise and serve you in the morn.
Reveal your presence to all who will gather in adoration and
    self-offering.
To those who cannot for good reason go gladly to your house,
give your strength and consolation so that they may know
of the concern of their community of faith.

Week Two, Day Fourteen

Make us receptive to your word for us, and enable us to know your will.
Bind your people together in a shared faith, a common witness, and compassionate service to the entire world,
through Christ Jesus, our savior and Lord.
Amen.

Anima Christi

Soul of Christ, sanctify me.
Body of Christ, save me.
Blood of Christ, inebriate me.
Water from the side of Christ, wash me.
Passion of Christ, strengthen me.
Oh good Jesus, hear me.
Within your wounds hide me.
Separated from you let me never be.
From the evil one protect me.
At the hour of my death call me,
and close to you bid me,
that with your saints
I may praise you forever and ever.
Amen.

Christ Be Near

Christ be near at either hand;
Christ behind, before me stand.
Christ with me where'er I go;
Christ around, above, below.

Christ be in my heart and mind;
Christ within my mind enshrined.
Christ control my wayward heart;
Christ abide and ne'er depart.
Christ my light and only way;

Christ my lantern night and day.
Christ be my unchanging friend,
guide and shepherd to the end.

Christ be all my strength and might,
Christ my captain for the flight.
Christ fulfill my mind's desire;
Christ, ennoble and inspire.

Christ the king and Lord of all,
find me ready at his call;
Christ receive my service whole,
hand and body, heart and mind.

Christ the king of kings descend,
and of tyrants make an end;
Christ on us and all below,
concord, love, and peace bestow.

Thanks to him, who for our food
gives his sacrifice flesh and blood;
praises to him unceasingly rise,
Christ whose glory fills the skies.

Covenant Prayer

I am no longer my own, but thine.
Put me to what thou will,
rank me with whom thou will.
Put me to doing, put me to suffering.
Let me be employed by thee or laid aside for thee,
exalted for thee or brought low for thee.
Let me be full, let me be empty.
Let me have all things, let me have nothing.
I freely and heartily yield all things
to thy good pleasure and disposal.

And now, oh glorious and blessed God,
Father, Son, and Holy Spirit,
thou art mine, and I am thine.
So be it.
And the covenant which I have made on earth,
let it be ratified in heaven.
Amen.

The Gloria

Glory to God in the highest,
And on earth peace to men of good will.
We praise you.
We bless you.
We adore you.
We glorify you.
We give you thanks for your great glory,
oh Lord God, heavenly king, God the Father almighty.
Oh Lord Jesus Christ, the only begotten Son,
oh Lord God, lamb of God, Son of the Father,
    you who take away the sins of the world, have mercy on us;
    you who take away the sins of the world, receive our prayer;
    you who sit at the right hand of the Father, have mercy on us.
For you alone are holy.
You alone are the Lord.
You alone, oh Jesus Christ, are the most high,
together with the Holy Spirit in the glory of God the Father.
Amen.

Glory Be

Glory be to the Father
and to the Son
and to the Holy Spirit;
as it was in the beginning,
is now,
and ever shall be,
world without end.
Amen.

WEEK THREE, DAY FIFTEEN

Today we take stock of where we are at this time of the month,
which is essentially halfway through now.
For example, what have I done in the past two weeks to help others?
What have I done in the last two weeks to alleviate
the larger concerns of human suffering?
What have I done in the last two weeks to seek justice,
to advance the humane treatment of all people?
What have I done in the last two weeks to overcome
the oppression and exploitation of the weak,
to speak up in defense of those who have been misrepresented
and mistreated?
Have I participated in weekly worship?
Have I received the Eucharist?
Have I been faithful in daily devotions?

Opening Prayer

Maker of all things, govern my life by your wisdom and council.
Forgive me plainly in those areas where I failed you
and strengthen me further where I have served you well.
Spare me from complacency or smugness over my spiritual successes.
Spare me also despair and guilt over my spiritual failures.
Grant to me in increasing measure the gift of your Spirit
so that I may grow in grace and more fully praise you day by day,
through Christ, who strengthens me.
Amen.

Prayer of Confession—Wash Me

See, oh merciful God, what return I,
your thankless servant, have made
for the innumerable favors

and the wonderful love you have shown me!
What wrongs I have done, what good left undone!
Wash away, I beg you, these faults and stains
with your precious blood, most kind redeemer,
and make up for my poverty by applying your merits.
Give me the protection I need to amend my life.
I give and surrender myself wholly to you,
and offer you all I possess,
with the prayer that you bestow your grace on me
so that I may be able to devote and employ
all the thinking power of my mind
and the strength of my body in your holy service,
who are God blessed for ever and ever.
Lord, enable me to see and find you in all things
and throughout my walks of life.
Amen.

Prayer for Illumination

Unfortunately, oh God, the eyes of my heart
are clouded over by the daily cares and fears of this world.
For the sake of your Spirit, restore my eyesight spiritually.
Cause the scales to fall from my eyes,
both through the study of your scriptures and through prayer.
Indeed, make your word be a lamp onto my feet and light unto
   my pathway,
through Christ, who is the true light and true vision.
Amen.

Week Three, Day Fifteen

Scripture Reading: Hebrews 13:15–16

Prayer of Exhortation

Oh God of great deeds,
on the first day of the week
    you magnificently called forth light out of darkness;
    you graciously raised Christ from the dead;
    you powerfully created the church through the gift of Spirit.
Through these three witnesses,
you testify to us concerning your covenant love.
Grant that all people who worship you this day
may do so in spirit and in truth
and may present to you a living sacrifice
of praise and thanksgiving;
we praise you for the signs of your love revealed in the bread and
    the cup.
By these gifts grant us not only hope until we gather again
but also graciousness that we may share with others the fruits of
    this earth,
through Christ, our savior and Lord.
Amen.

Anima Christi

Soul of Christ, sanctify me.
Body of Christ, save me.
Blood of Christ, inebriate me.
Water from the side of Christ, wash me.
Passion of Christ, strengthen me.
Oh good Jesus, hear me.
Within your wounds hide me.
Separated from you let me never be.
From the evil one protect me.
At the hour of my death call me,
and close to you bid me,

that with your saints
I may praise you forever and ever.
Amen.

Christ Be Near

Christ be near at either hand;
Christ behind, before me stand.
Christ with me where'er I go;
Christ around, above, below.

Christ be in my heart and mind;
Christ within my mind enshrined.
Christ control my wayward heart;
Christ abide and ne'er depart.

Christ my light and only way;
Christ my lantern night and day.
Christ be my unchanging friend,
guide and shepherd to the end.

Christ be all my strength and might,
Christ my captain for the flight.
Christ fulfill my mind's desire;
Christ, ennoble and inspire.

Christ the king and Lord of all,
find me ready at his call;
Christ receive my service whole,
hand and body, heart and mind.

Christ the king of kings descend,
and of tyrants make an end;
Christ on us and all below,
concord, love, and peace bestow.
Thanks to him, who for our food

gives his sacrifice flesh and blood;
praises to him unceasingly rise,
Christ whose glory fills the skies.

Covenant Prayer

I am no longer my own, but thine.
Put me to what thou will,
rank me with whom thou will.
Put me to doing, put me to suffering.
Let me be employed by thee or laid aside for thee,
exalted for thee or brought low for thee.
Let me be full, let me be empty.
Let me have all things, let me have nothing.
I freely and heartily yield all things
to thy good pleasure and disposal.
And now, oh glorious and blessed God,
Father, Son, and Holy Spirit,
thou art mine, and I am thine.
So be it.
And the covenant which I have made on earth,
let it be ratified in heaven.
Amen.

The Gloria

Glory to God in the highest,
And on earth peace to men of good will.
We praise you.
We bless you.
We adore you.
We glorify you.
We give you thanks for your great glory,
  oh Lord God, heavenly king, God the Father almighty.
Oh Lord Jesus Christ, the only begotten Son,

oh Lord God, lamb of God, Son of the Father,
    you who take away the sins of the world, have mercy on us;
    you who take away the sins of the world, receive our prayer;
    you who sit at the right hand of the Father, have mercy on us.
For you alone are holy.
You alone are the Lord.
You alone, oh Jesus Christ, are the most high,
together with the Holy Spirit in the glory of God the Father.
Amen.

Glory Be

Glory be to the Father
and to the Son
and to the Holy Spirit;
as it was in the beginning,
is now,
and ever shall be,
world without end.
Amen.

WEEK THREE, DAY SIXTEEN

Today we begin a consideration of the Beatitudes,
with the first being "Happy are the poor in spirit;
for theirs is the kingdom of heaven" (Matt 5:3, my translation).
The kingdom of heaven consists of mutuality as well as of grace.
We are thus commanded to alleviate the suffering of the
financially destitute as we ourselves have the ability to do so;
we are also called to assist the poor in spirit by sharing with them
whatever spiritual resources we ourselves have been given.
So therefore, both the poor in materiality and the poor in spirit
are in mind with this admonition.

Opening Prayer

Blessed God to the poor, from the riches of your grace
you share your bounty with all those who are in need.
Provide for the hungry and the homeless and teach us to do
    likewise
so that none may be prevented by physical circumstances
from loving and serving you with joy and strength.
So too provide all those who suffer poverty spiritually with
    sustenance
so that none may doubt your goodness or overlook your
    faithfulness.
Above all, prevent us from thinking that we are rich in spirit
    when, in fact,
we are wretched, pitiable, poor, blind, and naked.
We ask this through our Lord Christ Jesus who,
though he was rich, for our sakes became poor so that by his
    poverty,
we might become rich.
Amen.

Prayer of Confession—Wash Me

See, oh merciful God, what return I,
your thankless servant, have made
for the innumerable favors
and the wonderful love you have shown me!
What wrongs I have done, what good left undone!
Wash away, I beg you, these faults and stains
with your precious blood, most kind redeemer,
and make up for my poverty by applying your merits.
Give me the protection I need to amend my life.
I give and surrender myself wholly to you,
and offer you all I possess,
with the prayer that you bestow your grace on me
so that I may be able to devote and employ
all the thinking power of my mind
and the strength of my body in your holy service,
who are God blessed for ever and ever.
Lord, enable me to see and find you in all things
and throughout my walks of life.
Amen.

Prayer for Illumination

By the generosity of your heart, oh God,
you've given us evidence abundantly of your love.
So therefore, as the scriptures are read and pondered,
teach us that we do not rely on our own understanding
but only on that understanding that you have offered us instead,
through Christ, our teacher and redeemer.
Amen.

Week Three, Day Sixteen

Scripture Reading: Proverbs 2

Prayer of Exhortation

Remember, oh Lord, all for whom we prayed yesterday
while gathered together in corporate worship.
Teach us how best to serve them
with deeds of love and kindness.
Forgive us for those whom we neglected to raise up in prayer.
Help us to open our hearts to the needs of all.
Grant that what you taught us therein to do we may both ponder
  and perform.
Bind into one company of hope and one community of service
all that you have made and redeemed
by the sacrificial life and death of Jesus our Lord.
Amen.

Anima Christi

Soul of Christ, sanctify me.
Body of Christ, save me.
Blood of Christ, inebriate me.
Water from the side of Christ, wash me.
Passion of Christ, strengthen me.
Oh good Jesus, hear me.
Within your wounds hide me.
Separated from you let me never be.
From the evil one protect me.
At the hour of my death call me,
and close to you bid me,
that with your saints
I may praise you forever and ever.
Amen.

Christ Be Near

Christ be near at either hand;
Christ behind, before me stand.
Christ with me where'er I go;
Christ around, above, below.

Christ be in my heart and mind;
Christ within my mind enshrined.
Christ control my wayward heart;
Christ abide and ne'er depart.

Christ my light and only way;
Christ my lantern night and day.
Christ be my unchanging friend,
guide and shepherd to the end.

Christ be all my strength and might,
Christ my captain for the flight.
Christ fulfill my mind's desire;
Christ, ennoble and inspire.

Christ the king and Lord of all,
find me ready at his call;
Christ receive my service whole,
hand and body, heart and mind.

Christ the king of kings descend,
and of tyrants make an end;
Christ on us and all below,
concord, love, and peace bestow.

Thanks to him, who for our food
gives his sacrifice flesh and blood;
praises to him unceasingly rise,
Christ whose glory fills the skies.

Week Three, Day Sixteen

Covenant Prayer

I am no longer my own, but thine.
Put me to what thou will,
rank me with whom thou will.
Put me to doing, put me to suffering.
Let me be employed by thee or laid aside for thee,
exalted for thee or brought low for thee.
Let me be full, let me be empty.
Let me have all things, let me have nothing.
I freely and heartily yield all things
to thy good pleasure and disposal.
And now, oh glorious and blessed God,
Father, Son, and Holy Spirit,
thou art mine, and I am thine.
So be it.
And the covenant which I have made on earth,
let it be ratified in heaven.
Amen.

The Gloria

Glory to God in the highest,
And on earth peace to men of good will.
We praise you.
We bless you.
We adore you.
We glorify you.
We give you thanks for your great glory,
oh Lord God, heavenly king, God the Father almighty.
Oh Lord Jesus Christ, the only begotten Son,
oh Lord God, lamb of God, Son of the Father,
    you who take away the sins of the world, have mercy on us;
    you who take away the sins of the world, receive our prayer;
    you who sit at the right hand of the Father, have mercy on us.
For you alone are holy.

You alone are the Lord.
You alone, oh Jesus Christ, are the most high,
together with the Holy Spirit in the glory of God the Father.
Amen.

Glory Be

Glory be to the Father
and to the Son
and to the Holy Spirit;
as it was in the beginning,
is now,
and ever shall be,
world without end.
Amen.

WEEK THREE, DAY SEVENTEEN

Today we continue the discussion of the Beatitudes
with consideration specifically regarding those who mourn, and
 shall be comforted.
There can be two meanings of this Beatitude.
There are those who literally mourn, and for them the promise
of the resurrection is the great source of strength
because to comfort means "to make strong."
But there are also those—more figuratively—who regret their sins
and grieve over their errors.
God strengthens them also by the assurance of forgiveness.
Those who do mourn in fact, and in deed,
while turning to God, get strengthened.

Opening Prayer

Oh blessed God, you are a strong tower
and a sure defense in the time of trouble.
Without you, we have no certain help.
But you always come to us, pointing us to Mount Calvary
and to the empty tomb beyond it.
You are our gain in the time of loss, our forgiveness and direction
after we have erred and strayed like lost sheep.
To you be both praise and glory through Christ,
who strengthens us to do all things.
Amen.

Prayer of Confession—Wash Me

See, oh merciful God, what return I,
your thankless servant, have made
for the innumerable favors
and the wonderful love you have shown me!
What wrongs I have done, what good left undone!
Wash away, I beg you, these faults and stains

with your precious blood, most kind redeemer,
and make up for my poverty by applying your merits.
Give me the protection I need to amend my life.
I give and surrender myself wholly to you,
and offer you all I possess,
with the prayer that you bestow your grace on me
so that I may be able to devote and employ
all the thinking power of my mind
and the strength of my body in your holy service,
who are God blessed for ever and ever.
Lord, enable me to see and find you in all things
and throughout my walks of life.
Amen.

Prayer for Illumination

We await the strengthening power of your Word, oh God of hope.
Help us to remember your wonders of old,
to meditate on all your work both day and night,
so that we may be like trees planted about the streams of water,
which will yield their fruit in due season.
By the goodness of your Spirit, make us fruitful branches
as we ponder what you say to us now,
through Christ, who is the true vine and the tree of life.
Amen.

scripture Reading: Psalm 46:1–3

Prayer of Exhortation

Oh God, our rock and salvation, undergird us with your strength
lest we fall because we were trusting ourselves alone.
Assist with the Holy Spirit that we may abide in your love
and trust in your grace.
Spread upon us your transforming power;
overpower us with your goodwill and forgiveness

offered to us and all through Christ, our savior.
Amen.

Anima Christi

Soul of Christ, sanctify me.
Body of Christ, save me.
Blood of Christ, inebriate me.
Water from the side of Christ, wash me.
Passion of Christ, strengthen me.
Oh good Jesus, hear me.
Within your wounds hide me.
Separated from you let me never be.
From the evil one protect me.
At the hour of my death call me,
and close to you bid me,
that with your saints
I may praise you forever and ever.
Amen.

Christ Be Near

Christ be near at either hand;
Christ behind, before me stand.
Christ with me where'er I go;
Christ around, above, below.

Christ be in my heart and mind;
Christ within my mind enshrined.
Christ control my wayward heart;
Christ abide and ne'er depart.

Christ my light and only way;
Christ my lantern night and day.
Christ be my unchanging friend,

guide and shepherd to the end.

Christ be all my strength and might,
Christ my captain for the flight.
Christ fulfill my mind's desire;
Christ, ennoble and inspire.

Christ the king and Lord of all,
find me ready at his call;
Christ receive my service whole,
hand and body, heart and mind.

Christ the king of kings descend,
and of tyrants make an end;
Christ on us and all below,
concord, love, and peace bestow.

Thanks to him, who for our food
gives his sacrifice flesh and blood;
praises to him unceasingly rise,
Christ whose glory fills the skies.

Covenant Prayer

I am no longer my own, but thine.
Put me to what thou will,
rank me with whom thou will.
Put me to doing, put me to suffering.
Let me be employed by thee or laid aside for thee,
exalted for thee or brought low for thee.
Let me be full, let me be empty.
Let me have all things, let me have nothing.
I freely and heartily yield all things
to thy good pleasure and disposal.
And now, oh glorious and blessed God,
Father, Son, and Holy Spirit,

thou art mine, and I am thine.
So be it.
And the covenant which I have made on earth,
let it be ratified in heaven.
Amen.

The Gloria

Glory to God in the highest,
And on earth peace to men of good will.
We praise you.
We bless you.
We adore you.
We glorify you.
We give you thanks for your great glory,
oh Lord God, heavenly king, God the Father almighty.
Oh Lord Jesus Christ, the only begotten Son,
oh Lord God, lamb of God, Son of the Father,
    you who take away the sins of the world, have mercy on us;
    you who take away the sins of the world, receive our prayer;
    you who sit at the right hand of the Father, have mercy on us.
For you alone are holy.
You alone are the Lord.
You alone, oh Jesus Christ, are the most high,
together with the Holy Spirit in the glory of God the Father.
Amen.

Glory Be

Glory be to the Father
and to the Son
and to the Holy Spirit;
as it was in the beginning,
is now,
and ever shall be,
world without end.
Amen.

WEEK THREE, DAY EIGHTEEN

Today we continue the discussion of the Beatitudes
with consideration of meekness.
Jesus instructs us that happy are the gentle, for they shall inherit the earth.
Unfortunately, oftentimes meekness has been considered to be weakness.
However, meekness is better understood to be gentleness.
The meek will inherit the earth, not earn it;
this fact upends our usual values.

Opening Prayer

God, your thoughts are not our thoughts, and your ways are not our ways.
We confess to you our bewilderment of the quasi-strange values you treasure.
Transform us so drastically that we may embrace
your ways without fear of embarrassment.
Enable us to judge beyond what human eyes can see,
and what human ears can hear, so that you may regard us as the meek,
worthy inheritors of your mercy,
through Christ Jesus, in whom is true happiness.
Amen.

Prayer of Confession—Wash Me

See, oh merciful God, what return I,
your thankless servant, have made
for the innumerable favors
and the wonderful love you have shown me!
What wrongs I have done, what good left undone!
Wash away, I beg you, these faults and stains
with your precious blood, most kind redeemer,

and make up for my poverty by applying your merits.
Give me the protection I need to amend my life.
I give and surrender myself wholly to you,
and offer you all I possess,
with the prayer that you bestow your grace on me
so that I may be able to devote and employ
all the thinking power of my mind
and the strength of my body in your holy service,
who are God blessed for ever and ever.
Lord, enable me to see and find you in all things
and throughout my walks of life.
Amen.

Prayer for Illumination

Oh God, as we ponder you now,
by the grace of the Spirit, take away all the distractions of our minds.
Let no preoccupation with other matters
distract us from heeding your message,
from doing your work in our day in our place.
For making known your way to us, oh God,
we bless you, now and forever.
Amen.

scripture Reading: Colossians 3:12–15

Prayer of Exhortation

In the middle of this week, good Lord,
assure me again of your presence in the midst of life.
Renew my strength and determination to do your will on earth,
even as it is done in heaven.
Save me from both myself and foes, as well as contentment
and from a vision that is too narrow.
Enable me to reach beyond my parish, into my community;

Week Three, Day Eighteen

beyond my community, into every corner of your anguish world.
Help me to see even beyond this world
into the vast expenses of the universe
that was created by your might.
This I ask through Christ Jesus,
through whom all things were made,
and in whom all things hold together.
Amen.

Anima Christi

Soul of Christ, sanctify me.
Body of Christ, save me.
Blood of Christ, inebriate me.
Water from the side of Christ, wash me.
Passion of Christ, strengthen me.
Oh good Jesus, hear me.
Within your wounds hide me.
Separated from you let me never be.
From the evil one protect me.
At the hour of my death call me,
and close to you bid me,
that with your saints
I may praise you forever and ever.
Amen.

Christ Be Near

Christ be near at either hand;
Christ behind, before me stand.
Christ with me where'er I go;
Christ around, above, below.

Christ be in my heart and mind;
Christ within my mind enshrined.

Christ control my wayward heart;
Christ abide and ne'er depart.

Christ my light and only way;
Christ my lantern night and day.
Christ be my unchanging friend,
guide and shepherd to the end.

Christ be all my strength and might,
Christ my captain for the flight.
Christ fulfill my mind's desire;
Christ, ennoble and inspire.

Christ the king and Lord of all,
find me ready at his call;
Christ receive my service whole,
hand and body, heart and mind.

Christ the king of kings descend,
and of tyrants make an end;
Christ on us and all below,
concord, love, and peace bestow.

Thanks to him, who for our food
gives his sacrifice flesh and blood;
praises to him unceasingly rise,
Christ whose glory fills the skies.

Covenant Prayer

I am no longer my own, but thine.
Put me to what thou will,
rank me with whom thou will.
Put me to doing, put me to suffering.
Let me be employed by thee or laid aside for thee,
exalted for thee or brought low for thee.

Week Three, Day Eighteen

Let me be full, let me be empty.
Let me have all things, let me have nothing.
I freely and heartily yield all things
to thy good pleasure and disposal.
And now, oh glorious and blessed God,
Father, Son, and Holy Spirit,
thou art mine, and I am thine.
So be it.
And the covenant which I have made on earth,
let it be ratified in heaven.
Amen.

The Gloria

Glory to God in the highest,
And on earth peace to men of good will.
We praise you.
We bless you.
We adore you.
We glorify you.
We give you thanks for your great glory,
oh Lord God, heavenly king, God the Father almighty.
Oh Lord Jesus Christ, the only begotten Son,
oh Lord God, lamb of God, Son of the Father,
    you who take away the sins of the world, have mercy on us;
    you who take away the sins of the world, receive our prayer;
    you who sit at the right hand of the Father, have mercy on us.
For you alone are holy.
You alone are the Lord.
You alone, oh Jesus Christ, are the most high,
together with the Holy Spirit in the glory of God the Father.
Amen.

Glory Be

Glory be to the Father
and to the Son
and to the Holy Spirit;
as it was in the beginning,
is now,
and ever shall be,
world without end.
Amen.

WEEK THREE, DAY NINETEEN

Today we continue the discussion of the Beatitudes
with consideration of hungering and thirsting for what is right
   and just.
The apostle Paul instructs us as to whatever is true,
whatever is honorable, whatever is just, whatever is pure,
whatever is pleasing, whatever is commendable,
to think about those things (Phil 4:8).
God expects us to be famished for that which is right and just and
   honest.
Hungering and thirsting for what is right refers to being starved
for what is right, nothing more and nothing less.

Opening Prayer

To your people, oh Lord God, give a longing
for what is right insomuch as none of us can tolerate what is
   wrong.
What we must do, enable us to do with firmness and fairness,
without self-righteousness or pretentious wisdom.
Give us the grace to submit your correction when we are unjust
lest the things for which we stand be sullied by our own wrong-
   doing or inaction.
This we pray through Christ, our savior, whose ideals and deeds
   were never at odds.
Amen.

Prayer of Confession—Wash Me

See, oh merciful God, what return I,
your thankless servant, have made
for the innumerable favors
and the wonderful love you have shown me!
What wrongs I have done, what good left undone!
Wash away, I beg you, these faults and stains

with your precious blood, most kind redeemer,
and make up for my poverty by applying your merits.
Give me the protection I need to amend my life.
I give and surrender myself wholly to you,
and offer you all I possess,
with the prayer that you bestow your grace on me
so that I may be able to devote and employ
all the thinking power of my mind
and the strength of my body in your holy service,
who are God blessed for ever and ever.
Lord, enable me to see and find you in all things
and throughout my walks of life.
Amen.

Prayer for Illumination

Ever good God, as we open the pages of scripture,
open to us the breath of life, which is the cup of salvation,
that we may be satisfied
and share with others what you have shared with us,
through the one Christ Jesus, who is both provider and judge.
Amen.

scripture Reading: Psalm 42:1–2

Prayer of Exhortation

God, your glory calls your people to adoration daily.
Inspire all who plan to lead
in the worship of your congregation on the Lord's day.
Prepare my heart and the hearts of all your people
to receive their ministries with joy,
with gratitude to you,
and extravagant generosity toward others.
This we pray through Christ, the risen one.
Amen.

Week Three, Day Nineteen

Anima Christi

Soul of Christ, sanctify me.
Body of Christ, save me.
Blood of Christ, inebriate me.
Water from the side of Christ, wash me.
Passion of Christ, strengthen me.
Oh good Jesus, hear me.
Within your wounds hide me.
Separated from you let me never be.
From the evil one protect me.
At the hour of my death call me,
and close to you bid me,
that with your saints
I may praise you forever and ever.
Amen.

Christ Be Near

Christ be near at either hand;
Christ behind, before me stand.
Christ with me where'er I go;
Christ around, above, below.

Christ be in my heart and mind;
Christ within my mind enshrined.
Christ control my wayward heart;
Christ abide and ne'er depart.

Christ my light and only way;
Christ my lantern night and day.
Christ be my unchanging friend,
guide and shepherd to the end.

Christ be all my strength and might,
Christ my captain for the flight.
Christ fulfill my mind's desire;
Christ, ennoble and inspire.

Christ the king and Lord of all,
find me ready at his call;
Christ receive my service whole,
hand and body, heart and mind.

Christ the king of kings descend,
and of tyrants make an end;
Christ on us and all below,
concord, love, and peace bestow.

Thanks to him, who for our food
gives his sacrifice flesh and blood;
praises to him unceasingly rise,
Christ whose glory fills the skies.

Covenant Prayer

I am no longer my own, but thine.
Put me to what thou will,
rank me with whom thou will.
Put me to doing, put me to suffering.
Let me be employed by thee or laid aside for thee,
exalted for thee or brought low for thee.
Let me be full, let me be empty.
Let me have all things, let me have nothing.
I freely and heartily yield all things
to thy good pleasure and disposal.
And now, oh glorious and blessed God,
Father, Son, and Holy Spirit,
thou art mine, and I am thine.
So be it.

Week Three, Day Nineteen

And the covenant which I have made on earth,
let it be ratified in heaven.
Amen.

The Gloria

Glory to God in the highest,
And on earth peace to men of good will.
We praise you.
We bless you.
We adore you.
We glorify you.
We give you thanks for your great glory,
oh Lord God, heavenly king, God the Father almighty.
Oh Lord Jesus Christ, the only begotten Son,
oh Lord God, lamb of God, Son of the Father,
    you who take away the sins of the world, have mercy on us;
    you who take away the sins of the world, receive our prayer;
    you who sit at the right hand of the Father, have mercy on us.
For you alone are holy.
You alone are the Lord.
You alone, oh Jesus Christ, are the most high,
together with the Holy Spirit in the glory of God the Father.
Amen.

Glory Be

Glory be to the Father
and to the Son
and to the Holy Spirit;
as it was in the beginning,
is now,
and ever shall be,
world without end.
Amen.

WEEK THREE, DAY TWENTY

Today we continue the discussion of the Beatitudes
with consideration of mercy.
Jesus instructs us that happier are the merciful, for they shall be
 shown mercy.
We see here the reciprocity of the gospel:
we are to be merciful because God is merciful—even to our
 enemies.
On this day, it is wise for us to determine just
how much we have extended mercy to other people,
how we might use mercy more effectively,
and to whom we need to show mercy as a gift
so that they may understand more fully God's gracious gift of
 forgiveness.

Opening Prayer

God of all mercy and grace,
to us you extend forgiveness and help again and again.
Spare us from thinking that your mercies are automatic,
or that we must earn them.
Confront us with the mystery of your grace,
which is beyond all human conception.
In reflection of your mercy to us, cause us to be merciful
to other people in your name
so that those who see us may see beyond us to find you there
 behind us,
through Christ, who is mercy made flesh.
Amen.

Prayer of Confession—Wash Me

See, oh merciful God, what return I,
your thankless servant, have made
for the innumerable favors

Week Three, Day Twenty

and the wonderful love you have shown me!
What wrongs I have done, what good left undone!
Wash away, I beg you, these faults and stains
with your precious blood, most kind redeemer,
and make up for my poverty by applying your merits.
Give me the protection I need to amend my life.
I give and surrender myself wholly to you,
and offer you all I possess,
with the prayer that you bestow your grace on me
so that I may be able to devote and employ
all the thinking power of my mind
and the strength of my body in your holy service,
who are God blessed for ever and ever.
Lord, enable me to see and find you in all things
and throughout my walks of life.
Amen.

Prayer for Illumination

Oh Lord God, out of your loving-kindness
the scriptures have come so that in their testimony,
we may discover your ways.
By the power of your Spirit,
overcome the obstacles that we put in front of you.
Remove from us all threats, and in their place put love,
for perfect love casts out all fear,
through Christ Jesus, our Lord.
Amen.

scripture Reading: Hebrews 4:12–16

Prayer of Exhortation

On this day, Lord Jesus, the flesh which you took upon yourself for us,
and for our salvation, was hung upon the cross by us.

There you suffered all things and died that we might have life
and have it in the abundance.
Blessed are you, Lord Jesus, for your astounding and abounding
   grace,
who with the Father and in the Spirit is,
through all time and in all eternity, one God.
Amen.

Anima Christi

Soul of Christ, sanctify me.
Body of Christ, save me.
Blood of Christ, inebriate me.
Water from the side of Christ, wash me.
Passion of Christ, strengthen me.
Oh good Jesus, hear me.
Within your wounds hide me.
Separated from you let me never be.
From the evil one protect me.
At the hour of my death call me,
and close to you bid me,
that with your saints
I may praise you forever and ever.
Amen.

Week Three, Day Twenty

Christ Be Near

Christ be near at either hand;
Christ behind, before me stand.
Christ with me where'er I go;
Christ around, above, below.

Christ be in my heart and mind;
Christ within my mind enshrined.
Christ control my wayward heart;
Christ abide and ne'er depart.

Christ my light and only way;
Christ my lantern night and day.
Christ be my unchanging friend,
guide and shepherd to the end.

Christ be all my strength and might,
Christ my captain for the flight.
Christ fulfill my mind's desire;
Christ, ennoble and inspire.

Christ the king and Lord of all,
find me ready at his call;
Christ receive my service whole,
hand and body, heart and mind.

Christ the king of kings descend,
and of tyrants make an end;
Christ on us and all below,
concord, love, and peace bestow.

Thanks to him, who for our food
gives his sacrifice flesh and blood;
praises to him unceasingly rise,
Christ whose glory fills the skies.

Covenant Prayer

I am no longer my own, but thine.
Put me to what thou will,
rank me with whom thou will.
Put me to doing, put me to suffering.
Let me be employed by thee or laid aside for thee,
exalted for thee or brought low for thee.
Let me be full, let me be empty.
Let me have all things, let me have nothing.
I freely and heartily yield all things
to thy good pleasure and disposal.
And now, oh glorious and blessed God,
Father, Son, and Holy Spirit,
thou art mine, and I am thine.
So be it.
And the covenant which I have made on earth,
let it be ratified in heaven.
Amen.

The Gloria

Glory to God in the highest,
And on earth peace to men of good will.
We praise you.
We bless you.
We adore you.
We glorify you.
We give you thanks for your great glory,
oh Lord God, heavenly king, God the Father almighty.
Oh Lord Jesus Christ, the only begotten Son,
oh Lord God, lamb of God, Son of the Father,
    you who take away the sins of the world, have mercy on us;
    you who take away the sins of the world, receive our prayer;
    you who sit at the right hand of the Father, have mercy on us.
For you alone are holy.

Week Three, Day Twenty

You alone are the Lord.
You alone, oh Jesus Christ, are the most high,
together with the Holy Spirit in the glory of God the Father.
Amen.

Glory Be

Glory be to the Father
and to the Son
and to the Holy Spirit;
as it was in the beginning,
is now,
and ever shall be,
world without end.
Amen.

WEEK THREE, DAY TWENTY-ONE

Today we continue the discussion of the Beatitudes
with consideration of being pure in heart.
It has been said that purity of heart is to will one thing—unity of purpose.
The apostle Paul acknowledged that he wanted to do one thing
but often did another.
Ultimately, Paul resolved his conflict by noting that in his own power,
he cannot always be one mind;
only Christ could deliver him from spiritual confusion (Rom 7:21–25).
In the Psalms, it is noted that people must pray that God
might give them an undivided heart to revere his name (Ps 86:11).
We do well to pray for the same thing today.

Opening Prayer

Glorious God, you glow in the splendor that I cannot bear to see;
show me, however, as much as of yourself as I can behold.
Remove from me selfish motives.
I resolve with your help to remove from myself
all evil intentions that are mingled with holy desires.
Create in me a clean heart, oh God, and put a new spirit within me.
Only you—through Christ Jesus—can do this.
Amen.

Prayer of Confession—Wash Me

See, oh merciful God, what return I,
your thankless servant, have made
for the innumerable favors
and the wonderful love you have shown me!

Week Three, Day Twenty-One

What wrongs I have done, what good left undone!
Wash away, I beg you, these faults and stains
with your precious blood, most kind redeemer,
and make up for my poverty by applying your merits.
Give me the protection I need to amend my life.
I give and surrender myself wholly to you,
and offer you all I possess,
with the prayer that you bestow your grace on me
so that I may be able to devote and employ
all the thinking power of my mind
and the strength of my body in your holy service,
who are God blessed for ever and ever.
Lord, enable me to see and find you in all things
and throughout my walks of life.
Amen.

Prayer for Illumination

Oh Lord, let the words of my mouth and the meditations in my heart
be acceptable to you, insomuch as what I read and consider within my mind
may transform me outwardly,
through Christ, the Lord God, who is my rock and redeemer.
Amen.

scripture Reading: Psalm 19

Prayer of Exhortation

Prepare our hearts, oh Lord,
to join together with your whole congregation
to praise and serve you in the morn.
Reveal your presence to all who will gather in adoration and self-offering.
To those who cannot for good reason go gladly to your house,

give your strength and consolation so that they may know
of the concern of their community of faith.
Make us receptive to your word for us, and enable us to know your will.
Bind your people together in a shared faith, a common witness,
and compassionate service to the entire world,
through Christ Jesus, our savior and Lord.
Amen.

Anima Christi

Soul of Christ, sanctify me.
Body of Christ, save me.
Blood of Christ, inebriate me.
Water from the side of Christ, wash me.
Passion of Christ, strengthen me.
Oh good Jesus, hear me.
Within your wounds hide me.
Separated from you let me never be.
From the evil one protect me.
At the hour of my death call me,
and close to you bid me,
that with your saints
I may praise you forever and ever.
Amen.

Christ Be Near

Christ be near at either hand;
Christ behind, before me stand.
Christ with me where'er I go;
Christ around, above, below.

Christ be in my heart and mind;
Christ within my mind enshrined.

Week Three, Day Twenty-One

Christ control my wayward heart;
Christ abide and ne'er depart.

Christ my light and only way;
Christ my lantern night and day.
Christ be my unchanging friend,
guide and shepherd to the end.

Christ be all my strength and might,
Christ my captain for the flight.
Christ fulfill my mind's desire;
Christ, ennoble and inspire.

Christ the king and Lord of all,
find me ready at his call;
Christ receive my service whole,
hand and body, heart and mind.

Christ the king of kings descend,
and of tyrants make an end;
Christ on us and all below,
concord, love, and peace bestow.

Thanks to him, who for our food
gives his sacrifice flesh and blood;
praises to him unceasingly rise,
Christ whose glory fills the skies.

Covenant Prayer

I am no longer my own, but thine.
Put me to what thou will,
rank me with whom thou will.
Put me to doing, put me to suffering.
Let me be employed by thee or laid aside for thee,
exalted for thee or brought low for thee.

Let me be full, let me be empty.
Let me have all things, let me have nothing.
I freely and heartily yield all things
to thy good pleasure and disposal.
And now, oh glorious and blessed God,
Father, Son, and Holy Spirit,
thou art mine, and I am thine.
So be it.
And the covenant which I have made on earth,
let it be ratified in heaven.
Amen.

The Gloria

Glory to God in the highest,
And on earth peace to men of good will.
We praise you.
We bless you.
We adore you.
We glorify you.
We give you thanks for your great glory,
oh Lord God, heavenly king, God the Father almighty.
Oh Lord Jesus Christ, the only begotten Son,
oh Lord God, lamb of God, Son of the Father,
> you who take away the sins of the world, have mercy on us;
> you who take away the sins of the world, receive our prayer;
> you who sit at the right hand of the Father, have mercy on us.

For you alone are holy.
You alone are the Lord.
You alone, oh Jesus Christ, are the most high,
together with the Holy Spirit in the glory of God the Father.
Amen.

Week Three, Day Twenty-One

Glory Be

Glory be to the Father
and to the Son
and to the Holy Spirit;
as it was in the beginning,
is now,
and ever shall be,
world without end.
Amen.

WEEK FOUR, DAY TWENTY-TWO

Today we continue the discussion of the Beatitudes
with consideration of being peacemakers,
as though we were ambassadors for Christ himself.
Both Paul and Christ exhort us toward making peace with all comers.
One of the most popular Christian prayers begins
with the notion of "Lord, make me an instrument of your peace."
Peacemaking is more than mere passivity.
Instead, in truth, peacemaking is an active pursuit,
as is apparent through Christ's incarnation.

Opening Prayer

Oh God of wonders beyond our galaxy,
you are the author of peace and its most active proponent.
So greatly did you desire the reconciliation of all things
that you sent Christ into the world,
who assumed the humility of a mere servant,
as well as the humiliation of death by execution.
Grant us to risk comfort and status in the same manner as Jesus of Nazareth
in order that others may be at peace with you and with one another,
through Christ, who offers perfect peace to all comers.
Amen.

Prayer of Confession—Wash Me

See, oh merciful God, what return I,
your thankless servant, have made
for the innumerable favors
and the wonderful love you have shown me!
What wrongs I have done, what good left undone!
Wash away, I beg you, these faults and stains

Week Four, Day Twenty-Two

with your precious blood, most kind redeemer,
and make up for my poverty by applying your merits.
Give me the protection I need to amend my life.
I give and surrender myself wholly to you,
and offer you all I possess,
with the prayer that you bestow your grace on me
so that I may be able to devote and employ
all the thinking power of mys mind
and the strength of my body in your holy service,
who are God blessed for ever and ever.
Lord, enable me to see and find you in all things
and throughout my walks of life.
Amen.

Prayer for Illumination

By your tender mercies, oh Lord, and by the ministry of your
    Spirit,
open widely and clearly the meaning of your scriptures
so that in this time and place,
we made better understand how to heal your fractured world,
in Jesus' most holy name.
Amen.

scripture Reading: 2 Corinthians 5:16–21

Prayer of Exhortation

Oh God of great deeds,
on the first day of the week
    you magnificently called forth light out of darkness;
    you graciously raised Christ from the dead;
    you powerfully created the church through the gift of Spirit.

Through these three witnesses,
you testify to us concerning your covenant love.
Grant that all people who worship you this day
may do so in spirit and in truth
and may present to you a living sacrifice
of praise and thanksgiving;
we praise you for the signs of your love revealed in the bread and the cup.
By these gifts grant us not only hope until we gather again
but also graciousness that we may share with others the fruits of this earth,
through Christ, our savior and Lord.
Amen.

Anima Christi

Soul of Christ, sanctify me.
Body of Christ, save me.
Blood of Christ, inebriate me.
Water from the side of Christ, wash me.
Passion of Christ, strengthen me.
Oh good Jesus, hear me.
Within your wounds hide me.
Separated from you let me never be.
From the evil one protect me.
At the hour of my death call me,
and close to you bid me,
that with your saints
I may praise you forever and ever.
Amen.

Christ Be Near

Christ be near at either hand;
Christ behind, before me stand.

Week Four, Day Twenty-Two

Christ with me where'er I go;
Christ around, above, below.

Christ be in my heart and mind;
Christ within my mind enshrined.
Christ control my wayward heart;
Christ abide and ne'er depart.

Christ my light and only way;
Christ my lantern night and day.
Christ be my unchanging friend,
guide and shepherd to the end.

Christ be all my strength and might,
Christ my captain for the flight.
Christ fulfill my mind's desire;
Christ, ennoble and inspire.

Christ the king and Lord of all,
find me ready at his call;
Christ receive my service whole,
hand and body, heart and mind.

Christ the king of kings descend,
and of tyrants make an end;
Christ on us and all below,
concord, love, and peace bestow.

Thanks to him, who for our food
gives his sacrifice flesh and blood;
praises to him unceasingly rise,
Christ whose glory fills the skies.

Covenant Prayer

I am no longer my own, but thine.

Put me to what thou will,
rank me with whom thou will.
Put me to doing, put me to suffering.
Let me be employed by thee or laid aside for thee,
exalted for thee or brought low for thee.
Let me be full, let me be empty.
Let me have all things, let me have nothing.
I freely and heartily yield all things
to thy good pleasure and disposal.
And now, oh glorious and blessed God,
Father, Son, and Holy Spirit,
thou art mine, and I am thine.
So be it.
And the covenant which I have made on earth,
let it be ratified in heaven.
Amen.

The Gloria

Glory to God in the highest,
And on earth peace to men of good will.
We praise you.
We bless you.
We adore you.
We glorify you.
We give you thanks for your great glory,
oh Lord God, heavenly king, God the Father almighty.
Oh Lord Jesus Christ, the only begotten Son,
oh Lord God, lamb of God, Son of the Father,
> you who take away the sins of the world, have mercy on us;
> you who take away the sins of the world, receive our prayer;
> you who sit at the right hand of the Father, have mercy on us.

For you alone are holy.
You alone are the Lord.
You alone, oh Jesus Christ, are the most high,
together with the Holy Spirit in the glory of God the Father.

Week Four, Day Twenty-Two

Amen.

Glory Be

Glory be to the Father
and to the Son
and to the Holy Spirit;
as it was in the beginning,
is now,
and ever shall be,
world without end.
Amen.

WEEK FOUR, DAY TWENTY-THREE

Today we continue the discussion of the Beatitudes
with consideration of being persecuted for righteousness' sake.
Our urgent need is to see ourselves as our critics see us.
So then, when we are derided for the causes that we espouse,
it is well indeed to ask ourselves:
Is the object of our derision the cause I support
or my imperfect way of expressing that cause?
Further, do I want to see those who criticize me
persuaded and transformed or defeated and punished?
Moreover, how can I be faithful to what I believe
and at the same time be tender and compassionate to others?
The impurities of wrong motives for right actions
cannot exist in the kingdom of heaven.

Opening Prayer

Lord God, I see in you all who are unjustly accused
or wrongfully mistreated because of what they stand for.
To every person in that predicament
give the comfort of your presence now
and the assurance that they shall share in your triumph over evil
at the coming of your kingdom in its fullness,
through Jesus who—without thought for himself—
endured the ultimate persecution and achieved the final victory.
Amen.

Prayer of Confession—Wash Me

See, oh merciful God, what return I,
your thankless servant, have made
for the innumerable favors
and the wonderful love you have shown me!
What wrongs I have done, what good left undone!
Wash away, I beg you, these faults and stains

Week Four, Day Twenty-Three

with your precious blood, most kind redeemer,
and make up for my poverty by applying your merits.
Give me the protection I need to amend my life.
I give and surrender myself wholly to you,
and offer you all I possess,
with the prayer that you bestow your grace on me
so that I may be able to devote and employ
all the thinking power of my mind
and the strength of my body in your holy service,
who are God blessed for ever and ever.
Lord, enable me to see and find you in all things
and throughout my walks of life.
Amen.

Prayer for Illumination

Open to me now, oh gracious Lord, the mysteries of your grace
to the extent that I can know them,
and for all else, enable me to trust your goodness.
Amen.

Scripture Reading: 2 Timothy 3:10–15

Prayer of Exhortation

Remember, oh Lord, all for whom we prayed yesterday
while gathered together in corporate worship.
Teach us how best to serve them
with deeds of love and kindness.
Forgive us for those whom we neglected to raise up in prayer.
Help us to open our hearts to the needs of all.
Grant that what you taught us therein to do we may both ponder
    and perform.
Bind into one company of hope and one community of service
all that you have made and redeemed
by the sacrificial life and death of Jesus our Lord.

Amen.

Anima Christi

Soul of Christ, sanctify me.
Body of Christ, save me.
Blood of Christ, inebriate me.
Water from the side of Christ, wash me.
Passion of Christ, strengthen me.
Oh good Jesus, hear me.
Within your wounds hide me.
Separated from you let me never be.
From the evil one protect me.
At the hour of my death call me,
and close to you bid me,
that with your saints
I may praise you forever and ever.
Amen.

Christ Be Near

Christ be near at either hand;
Christ behind, before me stand.
Christ with me where'er I go;
Christ around, above, below.

Christ be in my heart and mind;
Christ within my mind enshrined.
Christ control my wayward heart;
Christ abide and ne'er depart.

Week Four, Day Twenty-Three

Christ my light and only way;
Christ my lantern night and day.
Christ be my unchanging friend,
guide and shepherd to the end.

Christ be all my strength and might,
Christ my captain for the flight.
Christ fulfill my mind's desire;
Christ, ennoble and inspire.

Christ the king and Lord of all,
find me ready at his call;
Christ receive my service whole,
hand and body, heart and mind.

Christ the king of kings descend,
and of tyrants make an end;
Christ on us and all below,
concord, love, and peace bestow.

Thanks to him, who for our food
gives his sacrifice flesh and blood;
praises to him unceasingly rise,
Christ whose glory fills the skies.

Covenant Prayer

I am no longer my own, but thine.
Put me to what thou will,
rank me with whom thou will.
Put me to doing, put me to suffering.
Let me be employed by thee or laid aside for thee,
exalted for thee or brought low for thee.
Let me be full, let me be empty.
Let me have all things, let me have nothing.
I freely and heartily yield all things

to thy good pleasure and disposal.
And now, oh glorious and blessed God,
Father, Son, and Holy Spirit,
thou art mine, and I am thine.
So be it.
And the covenant which I have made on earth,
let it be ratified in heaven.
Amen.

The Gloria

Glory to God in the highest,
And on earth peace to men of good will.
We praise you.
We bless you.
We adore you.
We glorify you.
We give you thanks for your great glory,
oh Lord God, heavenly king, God the Father almighty.
Oh Lord Jesus Christ, the only begotten Son,
oh Lord God, lamb of God, Son of the Father,
> you who take away the sins of the world, have mercy on us;
> you who take away the sins of the world, receive our prayer;
> you who sit at the right hand of the Father, have mercy on us.

For you alone are holy.
You alone are the Lord.
You alone, oh Jesus Christ, are the most high,
together with the Holy Spirit in the glory of God the Father.
Amen.

Week Four, Day Twenty-Three

Glory Be

Glory be to the Father
and to the Son
and to the Holy Spirit;
as it was in the beginning,
is now,
and ever shall be,
world without end.
Amen.

WEEK FOUR, DAY TWENTY-FOUR

Today's theme is life within the community.
It takes an entire congregation to nurture a Christian.
God has created human beings to be interlocked
in a system of relationships.
The church is a gift from God in order that we may
be provided with the community of faith in which to grow;
this community of faith spurs us onward in our pursuit of
 righteousness.

Opening Prayer

Oh God of hosts, you are never alone.
Even when you seem to be solitary, you live within the community of the Trinity;
likewise, you promise that we shall not be alone.
Increase our appreciation for the gift of your church,
and by the unifying power of your Spirit, bind us together
as a people who know themselves to be yours,
through Christ Jesus, whose promises we trust.
Amen.

Prayer of Confession—Wash Me

See, oh merciful God, what return I,
your thankless servant, have made
for the innumerable favors
and the wonderful love you have shown me!
What wrongs I have done, what good left undone!
Wash away, I beg you, these faults and stains
with your precious blood, most kind redeemer,
and make up for my poverty by applying your merits.
Give me the protection I need to amend my life.
I give and surrender myself wholly to you,
and offer you all I possess,

Week Four, Day Twenty-Four

with the prayer that you bestow your grace on me
so that I may be able to devote and employ
all the thinking power of my mind
and the strength of my body in your holy service,
who are God blessed for ever and ever.
Lord, enable me to see and find you in all things
and throughout my walks of life.
Amen.

Prayer for Illumination

By the same Spirit that worked among the original writers of scripture,
oh God, minister to us insomuch as what we read and ponder
may enliven us and stretch us through Christ, our savior and guide.
Amen.

scripture Reading: Galatians 6:1–10

Prayer of Exhortation

Oh God, our rock and salvation, undergird us with your strength
lest we fall because we were trusting ourselves alone.
Assist with the Holy Spirit that we may abide in your love
and trust in your grace.
Spread upon us your transforming power;
overpower us with your goodwill and forgiveness
offered to us and all through Christ, our savior.
Amen.

Anima Christi

Soul of Christ, sanctify me.
Body of Christ, save me.

Blood of Christ, inebriate me.
Water from the side of Christ, wash me.
Passion of Christ, strengthen me.
Oh good Jesus, hear me.
Within your wounds hide me.
Separated from you let me never be.
From the evil one protect me.
At the hour of my death call me,
and close to you bid me,
that with your saints
I may praise you forever and ever.
Amen.

Christ Be Near

Christ be near at either hand;
Christ behind, before me stand.
Christ with me where'er I go;
Christ around, above, below.

Christ be in my heart and mind;
Christ within my mind enshrined.
Christ control my wayward heart;
Christ abide and ne'er depart.

Christ my light and only way;
Christ my lantern night and day.
Christ be my unchanging friend,
guide and shepherd to the end.

Week Four, Day Twenty-Four

Christ be all my strength and might,
Christ my captain for the flight.
Christ fulfill my mind's desire;
Christ, ennoble and inspire.

Christ the king and Lord of all,
find me ready at his call;
Christ receive my service whole,
hand and body, heart and mind.

Christ the king of kings descend,
and of tyrants make an end;
Christ on us and all below,
concord, love, and peace bestow.

Thanks to him, who for our food
gives his sacrifice flesh and blood;
praises to him unceasingly rise,
Christ whose glory fills the skies.

Covenant Prayer

I am no longer my own, but thine.
Put me to what thou will,
rank me with whom thou will.
Put me to doing, put me to suffering.
Let me be employed by thee or laid aside for thee,
exalted for thee or brought low for thee.
Let me be full, let me be empty.
Let me have all things, let me have nothing.
I freely and heartily yield all things
to thy good pleasure and disposal.
And now, oh glorious and blessed God,
Father, Son, and Holy Spirit,
thou art mine, and I am thine.
So be it.

And the covenant which I have made on earth,
let it be ratified in heaven.
Amen.

The Gloria

Glory to God in the highest,
And on earth peace to men of good will.
We praise you.
We bless you.
We adore you.
We glorify you.
We give you thanks for your great glory,
oh Lord God, heavenly king, God the Father almighty.
Oh Lord Jesus Christ, the only begotten Son,
oh Lord God, lamb of God, Son of the Father,
    you who take away the sins of the world, have mercy on us;
    you who take away the sins of the world, receive our prayer;
    you who sit at the right hand of the Father, have mercy on us.
For you alone are holy.
You alone are the Lord.
You alone, oh Jesus Christ, are the most high,
together with the Holy Spirit in the glory of God the Father.
Amen.

Glory Be

Glory be to the Father
and to the Son
and to the Holy Spirit;
as it was in the beginning,
is now,
and ever shall be,
world without end.
Amen.

WEEK FOUR, DAY TWENTY-FIVE

Over the next four days, we consider the four characteristics
of the church set forth in the Nicene Creed:
"We believe in the one holy catholic and apostolic church."
Today we pray for the unity of Christ's church.
Because disagreements cause the world confusion,
at best, and at worst, scorn mixed with laughter,
to pray for the unity of the church is incumbent upon every
   Christian.

Opening Prayer

As you are one, oh God above, make the people of your new
   covenant one.
Help us to distinguish between what you deem to be
essential and what you consider to be merely convenient.
Help us to overcome differences and disagreements
in order to share the gospel message of reconciliation to all
   comers.
Bind up the wounds of your church and make it truly one body,
through Christ, who is its head.
Amen.

Prayer of Confession—Wash Me

See, oh merciful God, what return I,
your thankless servant, have made
for the innumerable favors
and the wonderful love you have shown me!
What wrongs I have done, what good left undone!
Wash away, I beg you, these faults and stains
with your precious blood, most kind redeemer,
and make up for my poverty by applying your merits.
Give me the protection I need to amend my life.
I give and surrender myself wholly to you,

and offer you all I possess,
with the prayer that you bestow your grace on me
so that I may be able to devote and employ
all the thinking power of my mind
and the strength of my body in your holy service,
who are God blessed for ever and ever.
Lord, enable me to see and find you in all things
and throughout my walks of life.
Amen.

Prayer for Illumination

Oh God of light and love,
send forth your Spirit to remove all obstacles
to the understanding and doing of your work
so that your goodness may be proclaimed by those who follow you.
Amen.

scripture Reading: Philippians 2:1–4

Prayer of Exhortation

In the middle of this week, good Lord,
assure me again of your presence in the midst of life.
Renew my strength and determination to do your will on earth,
even as it is done in heaven.
Save me from both myself and foes, as well as contentment
and from a vision that is too narrow.
Enable me to reach beyond my parish, into my community;
beyond my community, into every corner of your anguish world.
Help me to see even beyond this world
into the vast expenses of the universe
that was created by your might.
This I ask through Christ Jesus,
through whom all things were made,

Week Four, Day Twenty-Five

and in whom all things hold together.
Amen.

Anima Christi

Soul of Christ, sanctify me.
Body of Christ, save me.
Blood of Christ, inebriate me.
Water from the side of Christ, wash me.
Passion of Christ, strengthen me.
Oh good Jesus, hear me.
Within your wounds hide me.
Separated from you let me never be.
From the evil one protect me.
At the hour of my death call me,
and close to you bid me,
that with your saints
I may praise you forever and ever.
Amen.

Christ Be Near

Christ be near at either hand;
Christ behind, before me stand.
Christ with me where'er I go;
Christ around, above, below.

Christ be in my heart and mind;
Christ within my mind enshrined.
Christ control my wayward heart;
Christ abide and ne'er depart.

Christ my light and only way;
Christ my lantern night and day.
Christ be my unchanging friend,

guide and shepherd to the end.

Christ be all my strength and might,
Christ my captain for the flight.
Christ fulfill my mind's desire;
Christ, ennoble and inspire.

Christ the king and Lord of all,
find me ready at his call;
Christ receive my service whole,
hand and body, heart and mind.

Christ the king of kings descend,
and of tyrants make an end;
Christ on us and all below,
concord, love, and peace bestow.

Thanks to him, who for our food
gives his sacrifice flesh and blood;
praises to him unceasingly rise,
Christ whose glory fills the skies.

Covenant Prayer

I am no longer my own, but thine.
Put me to what thou will,
rank me with whom thou will.
Put me to doing, put me to suffering.
Let me be employed by thee or laid aside for thee,
exalted for thee or brought low for thee.
Let me be full, let me be empty.
Let me have all things, let me have nothing.
I freely and heartily yield all things
to thy good pleasure and disposal.
And now, oh glorious and blessed God,
Father, Son, and Holy Spirit,

Week Four, Day Twenty-Five

thou art mine, and I am thine.
So be it.
And the covenant which I have made on earth,
let it be ratified in heaven.
Amen.

The Gloria

Glory to God in the highest,
And on earth peace to men of good will.
We praise you.
We bless you.
We adore you.
We glorify you.
We give you thanks for your great glory,
oh Lord God, heavenly king, God the Father almighty.
Oh Lord Jesus Christ, the only begotten Son,
oh Lord God, lamb of God, Son of the Father,
    you who take away the sins of the world, have mercy on us;
    you who take away the sins of the world, receive our prayer;
    you who sit at the right hand of the Father, have mercy on us.
For you alone are holy.
You alone are the Lord.
You alone, oh Jesus Christ, are the most high,
together with the Holy Spirit in the glory of God the Father.
Amen.

Glory Be

Glory be to the Father
and to the Son
and to the Holy Spirit;
as it was in the beginning,
is now,
and ever shall be,
world without end.
Amen.

WEEK FOUR, DAY TWENTY-SIX

Today we consider what it means for the church to be holy.
To many people, the notion of being holy means
to be entirely good without flaw or fault.
However, holiness instead has to do with being set apart,
with being different from the world.
When God called one day of the week to be holy,
he meant that this day was to be set aside as different
from other days and distinctive in its practices.
The church, being holy, is called to live out in the world
ways of being and doing that are alternatives to
worldly standards and customs.
We are called to be holy,
not a club that panders to whatever is currently popular.

Opening Prayer

Oh blessed God, our help and our hope,
holy be your name, unlike every other name we know.
Holy be your ways, beyond the reach of earthly imperfection.
Holy be your people, called forth by you to show
the world a new way and a new hope.
Cause us to be what you call us to be,
through Christ Jesus, who died for being essentially different.
Amen.

Prayer of Confession—Wash Me

See, oh merciful God, what return I,
your thankless servant, have made
for the innumerable favors
and the wonderful love you have shown me!
What wrongs I have done, what good left undone!
Wash away, I beg you, these faults and stains
with your precious blood, most kind redeemer,

and make up for my poverty by applying your merits.
Give me the protection I need to amend my life.
I give and surrender myself wholly to you,
and offer you all I possess,
with the prayer that you bestow your grace on me
so that I may be able to devote and employ
all the thinking power of my mind
and the strength of my body in your holy service,
who are God blessed for ever and ever.
Lord, enable me to see and find you in all things
and throughout my walks of life.
Amen.

Prayer for Illumination

Oh Lord God, may we first have the reading of the word,
then silence in front of the word,
and then finally obedience to that word.
Amen.

scripture Reading: 1 Peter 1:15–16

Prayer of Exhortation

God, your glory calls your people to adoration daily.
Inspire all who plan to lead
in the worship of your congregation on the Lord's day.
Prepare my heart and the hearts of all your people
to receive their ministries with joy,
with gratitude to you,
and extravagant generosity toward others.
This we pray through Christ, the risen one.
Amen.

Week Four, Day Twenty-Six

Anima Christi

Soul of Christ, sanctify me.
Body of Christ, save me.
Blood of Christ, inebriate me.
Water from the side of Christ, wash me.
Passion of Christ, strengthen me.
Oh good Jesus, hear me.
Within your wounds hide me.
Separated from you let me never be.
From the evil one protect me.
At the hour of my death call me,
and close to you bid me,
that with your saints
I may praise you forever and ever.
Amen.

Christ Be Near

Christ be near at either hand;
Christ behind, before me stand.
Christ with me where'er I go;
Christ around, above, below.

Christ be in my heart and mind;
Christ within my mind enshrined.
Christ control my wayward heart;
Christ abide and ne'er depart.

Christ my light and only way;
Christ my lantern night and day.
Christ be my unchanging friend,
guide and shepherd to the end.

Christ be all my strength and might,
Christ my captain for the flight.
Christ fulfill my mind's desire;
Christ, ennoble and inspire.

Christ the king and Lord of all,
find me ready at his call;
Christ receive my service whole,
hand and body, heart and mind.

Christ the king of kings descend,
and of tyrants make an end;
Christ on us and all below,
concord, love, and peace bestow.

Thanks to him, who for our food
gives his sacrifice flesh and blood;
praises to him unceasingly rise,
Christ whose glory fills the skies.

Covenant Prayer

I am no longer my own, but thine.
Put me to what thou will,
rank me with whom thou will.
Put me to doing, put me to suffering.
Let me be employed by thee or laid aside for thee,
exalted for thee or brought low for thee.
Let me be full, let me be empty.
Let me have all things, let me have nothing.
I freely and heartily yield all things
to thy good pleasure and disposal.
And now, oh glorious and blessed God,
Father, Son, and Holy Spirit,
thou art mine, and I am thine.
So be it.

And the covenant which I have made on earth,
let it be ratified in heaven.
Amen.

The Gloria

Glory to God in the highest,
And on earth peace to men of good will.
We praise you.
We bless you.
We adore you.
We glorify you.
We give you thanks for your great glory,
oh Lord God, heavenly king, God the Father almighty.
Oh Lord Jesus Christ, the only begotten Son,
oh Lord God, lamb of God, Son of the Father,
    you who take away the sins of the world, have mercy on us;
    you who take away the sins of the world, receive our prayer;
    you who sit at the right hand of the Father, have mercy on us.
For you alone are holy.
You alone are the Lord.
You alone, oh Jesus Christ, are the most high,
together with the Holy Spirit in the glory of God the Father.
Amen.

Glory Be

Glory be to the Father
and to the Son
and to the Holy Spirit;
as it was in the beginning,
is now,
and ever shall be,
world without end.
Amen.

WEEK FOUR, DAY TWENTY-SEVEN

Today we consider what it means for the church to be catholic.
The true meaning of catholicity is the state of being universal.
So then, the church catholic entails the entirety of the church.
To affirm the catholicity of the church is to remind ourselves
that our brothers and sisters in the faith are scattered across
the entire earth, using various languages, literature, and customs.
When we dismiss the catholicity of the church,
we diminish our appreciation for the diversity of the Christian
    family at large.

Opening Prayer

Let all the people praise you, oh God of hosts,
for you have created all things and redeemed all things.
You have established a church, calling it to be faithful in every
    time and place.
Draw together all those who are in the church to be one in Christ
so that across the whole world, there may be witnesses to you,
to the glory of your name, oh blessed God,
who is one in diversity and three in unity.
Amen.

Prayer of Confession—Wash Me

See, oh merciful God, what return I,
your thankless servant, have made
for the innumerable favors
and the wonderful love you have shown me!
What wrongs I have done, what good left undone!
Wash away, I beg you, these faults and stains
with your precious blood, most kind redeemer,
and make up for my poverty by applying your merits.
Give me the protection I need to amend my life.
I give and surrender myself wholly to you,

Week Four, Day Twenty-Seven

and offer you all I possess,
with the prayer that you bestow your grace on me
so that I may be able to devote and employ
all the thinking power of my mind
and the strength of my body in your holy service,
who are God blessed for ever and ever.
Lord, enable me to see and find you in all things
and throughout my walks of life.
Amen.

Prayer for Illumination

In all times and places, oh dear God,
send for your Spirit to instruct your people so that the scriptures may come alive as they are read and pondered;
this we ask to Christ Jesus who is your Word made flesh.
Amen.

scripture Reading: Matthew 28:19–20

Prayer of Exhortation

On this day, Lord Jesus, the flesh which you took upon yourself for us,
and for our salvation, was hung upon the cross by us.
There you suffered all things and died that we might have life
and have it in the abundance.
Blessed are you, Lord Jesus, for your astounding and abounding grace,
who with the Father and in the Spirit is,
through all time and in all eternity, one God.
Amen.

Anima Christi

Soul of Christ, sanctify me.
Body of Christ, save me.
Blood of Christ, inebriate me.
Water from the side of Christ, wash me.
Passion of Christ, strengthen me.
Oh good Jesus, hear me.
Within your wounds hide me.
Separated from you let me never be.
From the evil one protect me.
At the hour of my death call me,
and close to you bid me,
that with your saints
I may praise you forever and ever.
Amen.

Christ Be Near

Christ be near at either hand;
Christ behind, before me stand.
Christ with me where'er I go;
Christ around, above, below.

Christ be in my heart and mind;
Christ within my mind enshrined.
Christ control my wayward heart;
Christ abide and ne'er depart.

Christ my light and only way;
Christ my lantern night and day.
Christ be my unchanging friend,
guide and shepherd to the end.

Week Four, Day Twenty-Seven

Christ be all my strength and might,
Christ my captain for the flight.
Christ fulfill my mind's desire;
Christ, ennoble and inspire.

Christ the king and Lord of all,
find me ready at his call;
Christ receive my service whole,
hand and body, heart and mind.

Christ the king of kings descend,
and of tyrants make an end;
Christ on us and all below,
concord, love, and peace bestow.

Thanks to him, who for our food
gives his sacrifice flesh and blood;
praises to him unceasingly rise,
Christ whose glory fills the skies.

Covenant Prayer

I am no longer my own, but thine.
Put me to what thou will,
rank me with whom thou will.
Put me to doing, put me to suffering.
Let me be employed by thee or laid aside for thee,
exalted for thee or brought low for thee.
Let me be full, let me be empty.
Let me have all things, let me have nothing.
I freely and heartily yield all things
to thy good pleasure and disposal.
And now, oh glorious and blessed God,
Father, Son, and Holy Spirit,
thou art mine, and I am thine.
So be it.

And the covenant which I have made on earth,
let it be ratified in heaven.
Amen.

The Gloria

Glory to God in the highest,
And on earth peace to men of good will.
We praise you.
We bless you.
We adore you.
We glorify you.
We give you thanks for your great glory,
oh Lord God, heavenly king, God the Father almighty.
Oh Lord Jesus Christ, the only begotten Son,
oh Lord God, lamb of God, Son of the Father,
    you who take away the sins of the world, have mercy on us;
    you who take away the sins of the world, receive our prayer;
    you who sit at the right hand of the Father, have mercy on us.
For you alone are holy.
You alone are the Lord.
You alone, oh Jesus Christ, are the most high,
together with the Holy Spirit in the glory of God the Father.
Amen.

Glory Be

Glory be to the Father
and to the Son
and to the Holy Spirit;
as it was in the beginning,
is now,
and ever shall be,
world without end.
Amen.

WEEK FOUR, DAY TWENTY-EIGHT

Today we consider what it means for the church to be apostolic.
An apostle is someone who is sent on a mission at its rudiment.
While oftentimes it is the case that the apostles referred only to
  the twelve plus Paul,
in truth it can well be argued that Mary Magdalene was also an
  apostle
since she was specifically sent by the risen Lord
to tell others that he had triumphed over death.
This further means that the church itself is apostolic,
for all Christians are sent into the world to proclaim the good
  news of Jesus Christ.
So then, we are sent in our own day—not to invent a new
  gospel—
to relay the gospel as laid down by the apostles instead.
We are not to find new gospel messages but rather
are asked to find new ways of proclaiming that old gospel,
which rings ever true.
This is why the content of the Bible is fixed
in recording the earliest message of Christ Jesus.
We are not free to add to the scripture our own experiences
as if they were also sacred history.
Nay, we are responsible to translate the old gospel into new wine
  skins.
This is what it means for the church to be apostolic.

Opening Prayer

To you, oh God, be all glory and honor.
From you, we have received grace upon grace.
To you, we owe all allegiance and gratitude.
In the midst of our temptations and distractions,
fasten our attention upon the faith we have received
from others and are called to share with others.
Make us your true apostles in and through Christ Jesus,

who both summons us and sends us.
Amen.

Prayer of Confession—Wash Me

See, oh merciful God, what return I,
your thankless servant, have made
for the innumerable favors
and the wonderful love you have shown me!
What wrongs I have done, what good left undone!
Wash away, I beg you, these faults and stains
with your precious blood, most kind redeemer,
and make up for my poverty by applying your merits.
Give me the protection I need to amend my life.
I give and surrender myself wholly to you,
and offer you all I possess,
with the prayer that you bestow your grace on me
so that I may be able to devote and employ
all the thinking power of my mind
and the strength of my body in your holy service,
who are God blessed for ever and ever.
Lord, enable me to see and find you in all things
and throughout my walks of life.
Amen.

Prayer for Illumination

Because it is your desire to be proclaimed throughout all the world,
oh holy God, grant us clarity of understanding as we search the scriptures
and teach us how best we can communicate their message
to those who know it not,
through Christ, our risen savior and Lord.
Amen.

Week Four, Day Twenty-Eight

Covenant Prayer

I am no longer my own, but thine.
Put me to what thou will,
rank me with whom thou will.
Put me to doing, put me to suffering.
Let me be employed by thee or laid aside for thee,
exalted for thee or brought low for thee.
Let me be full, let me be empty.
Let me have all things, let me have nothing.
I freely and heartily yield all things
to thy good pleasure and disposal.
And now, oh glorious and blessed God,
Father, Son, and Holy Spirit,
thou art mine, and I am thine.
So be it.
And the covenant which I have made on earth,
let it be ratified in heaven.
Amen.

The Gloria

Glory to God in the highest,
And on earth peace to men of good will.
We praise you.
We bless you.
We adore you.
We glorify you.
We give you thanks for your great glory,
oh Lord God, heavenly king, God the Father almighty.
Oh Lord Jesus Christ, the only begotten Son,
oh Lord God, lamb of God, Son of the Father,
    you who take away the sins of the world, have mercy on us;
    you who take away the sins of the world, receive our prayer;
    you who sit at the right hand of the Father, have mercy on us.
For you alone are holy.

You alone are the Lord.
You alone, oh Jesus Christ, are the most high,
together with the Holy Spirit in the glory of God the Father.
Amen.

Glory Be

Glory be to the Father
and to the Son
and to the Holy Spirit;
as it was in the beginning,
is now,
and ever shall be,
world without end.
Amen.

WEEK FIVE, DAY TWENTY-NINE

Today we consider the hope eternal.
The church of the New Testament always looks toward the future.
Indeed, it is the case that what we believe and hope for
should shape how we live in the present.
This is readily evident in our prayer to Jesus
that his will be done on earth as it is in heaven.
The hope in heaven is the firm conviction that
in spite of all the evils that beset us, God is in fact in charge,
and in the end, the triumph of God will be made clear,
and we will share in its glory.
In the meantime, the one holy catholic and apostolic church
is to live out on earth the hope to which it clings.
And insofar as possible, the church is to love the world
in the same way that God so loved the world.

Opening Prayer

Grant to me, oh gracious God, and all my brothers and sisters in Christ,
a strong sense of your steadfast love that we may see in what you promised us
both the firm hope for the future
as well as the pattern of life that we can follow in the present,
through Christ, our Lord.
Amen.

Prayer of Confession—Wash Me

See, oh merciful God, what return I,
your thankless servant, have made
for the innumerable favors
and the wonderful love you have shown me!
What wrongs I have done, what good left undone!
Wash away, I beg you, these faults and stains

with your precious blood, most kind redeemer,
and make up for my poverty by applying your merits.
Give me the protection I need to amend my life.
I give and surrender myself wholly to you,
and offer you all I possess,
with the prayer that you bestow your grace on me
so that I may be able to devote and employ
all the thinking power of my mind
and the strength of my body in your holy service,
who are God blessed for ever and ever.
Lord, enable me to see and find you in all things
and throughout my walks of life.
Amen.

Prayer for Illumination

Oh God above us all, you are the help and confidence of all who seek you:
without your aid, we cannot understand the scriptures
—with eyes that do not see, with ears that do not hear, and with a heart that will not learn or love.
Open our eyes and hearts and minds,
and cause us to know inwardly what you present to us outwardly,
through Christ Jesus, who opens doors that no one can shut.
Amen.

scripture Reading: Titus 1:1–3

Prayer of Exhortation

Oh God of great deeds,
on the first day of the week
    you magnificently called forth light out of darkness;
    you graciously raised Christ from the dead;
    you powerfully created the church through the gift of Spirit.
Through these three witnesses,

Week Five, Day Twenty-Nine

you testify to us concerning your covenant love.
Grant that all people who worship you this day
may do so in spirit and in truth
and may present to you a living sacrifice
of praise and thanksgiving;
we praise you for the signs of your love revealed in the bread and
   the cup.
By these gifts grant us not only hope until we gather again
but also graciousness that we may share with others the fruits of
   this earth,
through Christ, our savior and Lord.
Amen.

Anima Christi

Soul of Christ, sanctify me.
Body of Christ, save me.
Blood of Christ, inebriate me.
Water from the side of Christ, wash me.
Passion of Christ, strengthen me.
Oh good Jesus, hear me.
Within your wounds hide me.
Separated from you let me never be.
From the evil one protect me.
At the hour of my death call me,
and close to you bid me,
that with your saints
I may praise you forever and ever.
Amen.

Christ Be Near

Christ be near at either hand;
Christ behind, before me stand.
Christ with me where'er I go;
Christ around, above, below.

Christ be in my heart and mind;
Christ within my mind enshrined.
Christ control my wayward heart;
Christ abide and ne'er depart.

Christ my light and only way;
Christ my lantern night and day.
Christ be my unchanging friend,
guide and shepherd to the end.

Christ be all my strength and might,
Christ my captain for the flight.
Christ fulfill my mind's desire;
Christ, ennoble and inspire.

Christ the king and Lord of all,
find me ready at his call;
Christ receive my service whole,
hand and body, heart and mind.

Christ the king of kings descend,
and of tyrants make an end;
Christ on us and all below,
concord, love, and peace bestow.

Thanks to him, who for our food
gives his sacrifice flesh and blood;
praises to him unceasingly rise,
Christ whose glory fills the skies.

Week Five, Day Twenty-Nine

Covenant Prayer

I am no longer my own, but thine.
Put me to what thou will,
rank me with whom thou will.
Put me to doing, put me to suffering.
Let me be employed by thee or laid aside for thee,
exalted for thee or brought low for thee.
Let me be full, let me be empty.
Let me have all things, let me have nothing.
I freely and heartily yield all things
to thy good pleasure and disposal.
And now, oh glorious and blessed God,
Father, Son, and Holy Spirit,
thou art mine, and I am thine.
So be it.
And the covenant which I have made on earth,
let it be ratified in heaven.
Amen.

The Gloria

Glory to God in the highest,
And on earth peace to men of good will.
We praise you.
We bless you.
We adore you.
We glorify you.
We give you thanks for your great glory,
oh Lord God, heavenly king, God the Father almighty.
Oh Lord Jesus Christ, the only begotten Son,
oh Lord God, lamb of God, Son of the Father,
    you who take away the sins of the world, have mercy on us;
    you who take away the sins of the world, receive our prayer;
    you who sit at the right hand of the Father, have mercy on us.
For you alone are holy.

You alone are the Lord.
You alone, oh Jesus Christ, are the most high,
together with the Holy Spirit in the glory of God the Father.
Amen.

Glory Be

Glory be to the Father
and to the Son
and to the Holy Spirit;
as it was in the beginning,
is now,
and ever shall be,
world without end.
Amen.

WEEK FIVE, DAY THIRTY

Today we consider thanksgiving to God in word and in deed.
Ingratitude is a grave offense toward God,
and unfortunately the closer to God we think we are,
the more inclined we are to take divine grace for granted.
As this month comes to close, we should ask ourselves this:
For what experiences in the past month have we particularly praised God?
Moreover, what opportunities for thanksgiving have we overlooked during this month?
Have we shown gratitude in word only or also by deed,
particularly by demonstrating concern for the weak, the lowly, and the suffering?

Opening Prayer

Bless the Lord, oh my soul.
All that is within me, bless God's holy name.
For you, oh God, have showered me with blessings too numerous to count;
in return, too often have I overlooked, or taken for granted, your bounty.
Beyond all else you've given, grant me yet one more thing:
an unfailingly grateful heart.
Amen.

Prayer of Confession—Wash Me

See, oh merciful God, what return I,
your thankless servant, have made
for the innumerable favors
and the wonderful love you have shown me!
What wrongs I have done, what good left undone!
Wash away, I beg you, these faults and stains
with your precious blood, most kind redeemer,

and make up for my poverty by applying your merits.
Give me the protection I need to amend my life.
I give and surrender myself wholly to you,
and offer you all I possess,
with the prayer that you bestow your grace on me
so that I may be able to devote and employ
all the thinking power of my mind
and the strength of my body in your holy service,
who are God blessed for ever and ever.
Lord, enable me to see and find you in all things
and throughout my walks of life.
Amen.

Prayer for Illumination

Oh blessed Lord God, there is nowhere that you are not.
You fill every crevice of the universe.
Infiltrate my whole being with your grace
so that the reading and study of your word will leave
no part of me as exempt from seeking and serving you,
through Christ, who is all and in all.
Amen.

scripture Reading: 1 Thessalonians 5:12–22

Prayer of Exhortation

Remember, oh Lord, all for whom we prayed yesterday
while gathered together in corporate worship.
Teach us how best to serve them
with deeds of love and kindness.
Forgive us for those whom we neglected to raise up in prayer.
Help us to open our hearts to the needs of all.
Grant that what you taught us therein to do we may both ponder
    and perform.
Bind into one company of hope and one community of service

all that you have made and redeemed
by the sacrificial life and death of Jesus our Lord.
Amen.

Anima Christi

Soul of Christ, sanctify me.
Body of Christ, save me.
Blood of Christ, inebriate me.
Water from the side of Christ, wash me.
Passion of Christ, strengthen me.
Oh good Jesus, hear me.
Within your wounds hide me.
Separated from you let me never be.
From the evil one protect me.
At the hour of my death call me,
and close to you bid me,
that with your saints
I may praise you forever and ever.
Amen.

Christ Be Near

Christ be near at either hand;
Christ behind, before me stand.
Christ with me where'er I go;
Christ around, above, below.

Christ be in my heart and mind;
Christ within my mind enshrined.
Christ control my wayward heart;
Christ abide and ne'er depart.

Christ my light and only way;
Christ my lantern night and day.

Christ be my unchanging friend,
guide and shepherd to the end.

Christ be all my strength and might,
Christ my captain for the flight.
Christ fulfill my mind's desire;
Christ, ennoble and inspire.

Christ the king and Lord of all,
find me ready at his call;
Christ receive my service whole,
hand and body, heart and mind.

Christ the king of kings descend,
and of tyrants make an end;
Christ on us and all below,
concord, love, and peace bestow.

Thanks to him, who for our food
gives his sacrifice flesh and blood;
praises to him unceasingly rise,
Christ whose glory fills the skies.

Covenant Prayer

I am no longer my own, but thine.
Put me to what thou will,
rank me with whom thou will.
Put me to doing, put me to suffering.
Let me be employed by thee or laid aside for thee,
exalted for thee or brought low for thee.
Let me be full, let me be empty.
Let me have all things, let me have nothing.
I freely and heartily yield all things
to thy good pleasure and disposal.
And now, oh glorious and blessed God,

Father, Son, and Holy Spirit,
thou art mine, and I am thine.
So be it.
And the covenant which I have made on earth,
let it be ratified in heaven.
Amen.

The Gloria

Glory to God in the highest,
And on earth peace to men of good will.
We praise you.
We bless you.
We adore you.
We glorify you.
We give you thanks for your great glory,
oh Lord God, heavenly king, God the Father almighty.
Oh Lord Jesus Christ, the only begotten Son,
oh Lord God, lamb of God, Son of the Father,
>you who take away the sins of the world, have mercy on us;
>you who take away the sins of the world, receive our prayer;
>you who sit at the right hand of the Father, have mercy on us.

For you alone are holy.
You alone are the Lord.
You alone, oh Jesus Christ, are the most high,
together with the Holy Spirit in the glory of God the Father.
Amen.

Glory Be

Glory be to the Father
and to the Son
and to the Holy Spirit;
as it was in the beginning,
is now,
and ever shall be,
world without end.
Amen.

WEEK FIVE, FINAL DAY

Today we consider our end of the month examination.
Fasting is the proper way that we might note our
devotion to God on this final day of the month.
Fasting could be either as traditionally understood,
by not taking any food for the day,
but it could also mean abstaining from watching TV, for example.
Our obedience to God causes us to examine ourselves
and only then to eat the bread and drink the cup of the Eucharist,
for all who eat and drink without discerning the body,
eat and drink judgment against themselves.

Opening Prayer

Give me honesty and integrity, oh Lord God,
so that I may carefully probe my actions and my motivations,
with the view to reforming those that are in need of remedy.
Help me to put aside self-deception and defensiveness,
and to acknowledge that I am indeed a sinner,
yet one who knows the power of grace and covets the joy of
    transformation.
Search me, oh God, and know my heart,
and lead me in the way everlasting,
through Christ, who died for our sins and rose again for our
    justification.
Amen.

Prayer of Confession—Wash Me

See, oh merciful God, what return I,
your thankless servant, have made
for the innumerable favors
and the wonderful love you have shown me!
What wrongs I have done, what good left undone!
Wash away, I beg you, these faults and stains

with your precious blood, most kind redeemer,
and make up for my poverty by applying your merits.
Give me the protection I need to amend my life.
I give and surrender myself wholly to you,
and offer you all I possess,
with the prayer that you bestow your grace on me
so that I may be able to devote and employ
all the thinking power of my mind
and the strength of my body in your holy service,
who are God blessed for ever and ever.
Lord, enable me to see and find you in all things
and throughout my walks of life.
Amen.

Prayer for Illumination

Oh blessed God, show me through the scriptures
both your judgment as well as your grace
that I may be neither self-satisfied nor terrified.
Enable me to accept Jesus as both my example
and the redeemer of all my sin;
for to him and through him and in him I do pray.
Amen.

scripture Reading: 1 Corinthians 11:28–29

Prayer of Exhortation

Oh blessed God, mercifully forgive the wrong that I have done
and the good that I have neglected to do.
Let not your forgiveness be used by me as an excuse
to continue in my old, unredeemed ways.
Rather, let your kindness alter what I am and what I do.
Restore in me the image of yourself with which you endowed me
  in my re-creation.
Have mercy upon me, Lord, a sinner;

Week Five, Final Day

Christ, have mercy upon me, a penitent.
Lord, have mercy upon me, and make me whole.
Amen.

Anima Christi

Soul of Christ, sanctify me.
Body of Christ, save me.
Blood of Christ, inebriate me.
Water from the side of Christ, wash me.
Passion of Christ, strengthen me.
Oh good Jesus, hear me.
Within your wounds hide me.
Separated from you let me never be.
From the evil one protect me.
At the hour of my death call me,
and close to you bid me,
that with your saints
I may praise you forever and ever.
Amen.

Christ Be Near

Christ be near at either hand;
Christ behind, before me stand.
Christ with me where'er I go;
Christ around, above, below.

Christ be in my heart and mind;
Christ within my mind enshrined.
Christ control my wayward heart;
Christ abide and ne'er depart.

Christ my light and only way;
Christ my lantern night and day.
Christ be my unchanging friend,
guide and shepherd to the end.

Christ be all my strength and might,
Christ my captain for the flight.
Christ fulfill my mind's desire;
Christ, ennoble and inspire.

Christ the king and Lord of all,
find me ready at his call;
Christ receive my service whole,
hand and body, heart and mind.

Christ the king of kings descend,
and of tyrants make an end;
Christ on us and all below,
concord, love, and peace bestow.

Thanks to him, who for our food
gives his sacrifice flesh and blood;
praises to him unceasingly rise,
Christ whose glory fills the skies.

Covenant Prayer

I am no longer my own, but thine.
Put me to what thou will,
rank me with whom thou will.
Put me to doing, put me to suffering.
Let me be employed by thee or laid aside for thee,
exalted for thee or brought low for thee.
Let me be full, let me be empty.
Let me have all things, let me have nothing.
I freely and heartily yield all things

Week Five, Final Day

to thy good pleasure and disposal.
And now, oh glorious and blessed God,
Father, Son, and Holy Spirit,
thou art mine, and I am thine.
So be it.
And the covenant which I have made on earth,
let it be ratified in heaven.
Amen.

The Gloria

Glory to God in the highest,
And on earth peace to men of good will.
We praise you.
We bless you.
We adore you.
We glorify you.
We give you thanks for your great glory,
oh Lord God, heavenly king, God the Father almighty.
Oh Lord Jesus Christ, the only begotten Son,
oh Lord God, lamb of God, Son of the Father,
    you who take away the sins of the world, have mercy on us;
    you who take away the sins of the world, receive our prayer;
    you who sit at the right hand of the Father, have mercy on us.
For you alone are holy.
You alone are the Lord.
You alone, oh Jesus Christ, are the most high,
together with the Holy Spirit in the glory of God the Father.
Amen.

Glory Be

Glory be to the Father
and to the Son
and to the Holy Spirit;
as it was in the beginning,
is now,
and ever shall be,
world without end.
Amen.

www.ingramcontent.com/pod-product-compliance
Lightning Source LLC
Chambersburg PA
CBHW051057160426
43193CB00010B/1218